JUNE GUSTAFSON MUNRO, MA
ILLUSTRATED BY ANDREW D. MUNRO

MOVEMENT EDUCATION

A Program for Young Children

Ages 2 to 7

MDEA PRESS
Newport News, Virginia
Orinda, California

Library of Congress Cataloging in Publication Data
Munro, June Gustafson, 1941 -
    Movement education.

    Bibliography: p.
    Includes index.
    1. Movement education—United States. 2. Movement
education—Study and teaching—United States.   1. Title.
GV452.M86   1985   372.8'6044   85-62484
ISBN 0-9611820-0-8

Cover Design © by Jean D. Bowman
Illustrations © by Andrew D. Munro

Library of Congress Catalog Number 85-62484
ISBN 0-9611820-08

MDEA Press
79 Knollwood Drive, Newport News, Virginia 23602
55 Charles Hill Road, Orinda, California 94563

Things You Need To Know

MOVEMENT EDUCATION: A PROGRAM FOR YOUNG CHILDREN AGES 2 TO 7 was originally written as my masters thesis project and then published especially for preschool age children and their teachers to fill the need for a sequential, creative, movement education program which included an assessment of basic movement skills. The original book has been expanded and republished to include all children who are developing their fundamental movement skills.

Children develop their fundamental movement skills between the ages of 2 and 7. Initially they explore and gain experience with body awareness, balance, locomotion, spatial relationships, manipulation and rhythm and timing. With continued movement experiences children ages 4 and 5 become increasingly proficient at more mature levels. By the ages of 6 and 7 children are able to combine and integrate fundamental movement skills into well coordinated acts which can then be applied to dance, recreational activities as well as competitive sports for both individual and group enjoyment.

Movement activities enhance children's cognitive and affective development as well as their physical skills. Younger children can gain experience with colors, shapes, sequencing, auditory memory and curriculum themes while older children can benefit from the use of names, letters, words, numbers and math problems when these are combined with movement activities. For example, children can bowl at "pins", marked with numerals, choose a piece of colored paper and then add up or subtract their own scores. This activity can also be done using letters to be made into words or with words to form sentences.

Movement activities which are designed to foster success for each child enhance his or her self-esteem. For example, in throwing bean bags at a target, three throwing places can be marked on the floor, allowing each child to choose the point from which he or she can be most successful yet still be challenged. Another example is to design one target to insure success for children of different abilities. A large target of poster board which contains smaller targets allows each child to be successful by hitting the large poster board itself or one of the smaller targets. Children who are successful and yet challenged feel good about themselves. Adults working with young children can facilitate their movement success by encouraging them to explore and "try out" all the possible muscular responses of which their bodies and imagination are are capable. By valuing children's own ideas and original movement solutions, adults enhance the children's self-esteem.

All children benefit from using all of their senses during movement activities. Because the activities in this book are multi-sensory in nature, they can be used with children of many different special needs and learning styles or, if needed, these activities can be easily adapted for a student's individual educational program (IEP).

Movement education activities are non-sexist and multicultural. Girls and boys participate with equal success in the same activities. Children of all cultural backgrounds are valued. Each child's ideas, name and culture become an important part of movement activities. For example, a Chinese dragon parade, with oriental music, can be used as an activity for coordination, rhythm and timing or common space. Using music of many cultures benefits all children, while increasing the self-esteem in those children from each culture whose music is heard.

The activities in this book are valuable for children in many settings: school, preschool, day care, after-school and recreational programs, gifted and special education, pre-dance and pre-gymnastics classes, hospital settings, camps and "at home" with parents or primary care-givers. These activities can be used during movement time, music time, on the playground, as a suppliment to the P.E. program and after recess to "center" the children. Teachers, aides, nurses, recreational specialists, parents and college students can use MOVEMENT EDUCATION: A PROGRAM FOR YOUNG CHILDREN AGES 2 TO 7 with enjoyment and success whether working independently or in a team teaching situation.

Participation in fundamental movement activities which are multi-sensory, non-sexist, multicultural and success oriented help children develop to their full potential—a worthy goal for all adults working with young children!

Have fun!

June Gustafson Munro
MDEA Press, 1985

Acknowledgements

I wish to thank Peek Publications for its permission to use material from **PERCEPTUAL-MOTOR LEARNING—Theory and Practice** by Lerch, et al. Copyright 1974 by Peek Publications, P.O. Box 50123, Palo Alto, CA 24303. I also wish to thank Charles C. Thomas, Publisher for his permission to use material from **MOTOR DEVELOPMENT IN THE PRESCHOOL YEARS** by Skinner. Copyright 1979 by Charles C. Thomas, Publisher, 2600 South First Street, Springfield, Illinois 62717. If any material has been used inadvertently, without due credit, correction will be made in future copies.

This book would not have been written without the early encouragement and continued insight, input, support and friendship from Nancy Drake. I also wish to thank the teachers at Walnut Avenue Community Preschool in Walnut Creek, California, for their creative ideas and suggestions while implementing and evaluating the program. My thanks goes to Peggy Beltramo who cheerfully typed so many drafts, to Pam Sommers for proof reading, and to Rosemary Peterson and Beverly Casebeer for their editorial assistance.

Special thanks goes to Bob Hewes and David Munro for their patience, encouragement and practical assistance while revising and expanding this book. The illustrations are a product of many fun hours working with Andrew Munro, capturing joyful yet accurate movement, and the covers are the result of many pleasant sessions working with Jean Dudley Bowman at the old Chamberlin Hotel, overlooking Hampton Roads. I am grateful to these two talented artists!

My very special thanks and love go to my husband David, and our sons, Drew and Robbie, for their encouragement and assuming so many household responsibilities for so long, and to my parents, Norman and Betty Gustafson, who always believe in me!

J.G.M.

Dedication

This book was inspired by my son, Robert, whose visual impairment as a baby redirected his learning through his other senses. During the years, he has learned the joy of movement, developed and used his fundamental movement skills and gained in self-confidence. From first learning to climb our kitchen stool in order to get to and eat freshly baked bread, to breaking two front teeth and his brother's bike in order to win a race, to becoming an accomplished swimmer, rollerskater and downhill skier, Robbie has taught me that joy and self-confidence result as children develop their full potential—including their physical potential.

Many thanks go to all of Robbie's wonderful teachers, mobility instructors, recreational specialists and Scout leaders for helping him develop so well, to his many terrific friends throughout the country, and especially to Robbie for his delightful sense of humor and for being himself!

J.G.M.

TABLE OF CONTENTS

INTRODUCTION

A RATIONALE FOR PRESCHOOL

MOVEMENT EDUCATION

I hear and I forget
I see and I remember
I do and I understand.

--Chinese Proverb

Movement is of vital interest to young children and important in developing their full potential. In fact, movement enters into all facets of children's development: physical, affective and cognitive, particularly during the early childhood years. These are the years when children are <u>learning to move</u> as well as <u>moving to learn</u>; movement and learning go hand in hand. Enhancing children's ability to move effectively, with control and joy is a worthy goal of every preschool curriculum.

<u>Learning to move</u> involves the continuous development of children's fundamental movement abilities: walking, running, jumping, skipping, rolling, throwing, catching, kicking, stretching, bending, twisting and shaking. A good sense of balance, rhythm and coordination are essential for success in these activities. Later, between the ages of 6 and 10 years, children apply fundamental movement skills in a general way to sports, games and dancing. Children should

be exposed to a wide variety of fundamental movements and be encouraged to refine them.

Maturation alone will not account for the development of mature, efficient movement patterns. Children need to have experiences in all of the movement areas in order to maximize their full potential. President Dwight Eisenhower established the President's Council on Youth Fitness in 1956, to promote the upgrading of the physical fitness of our children when the results of the Kraus-Hirshland study showed that American children were often found to be in poor physical condition as compared to European children. The President's Council promoted the importance of movement, motor development and good physical education programs as a means of enhancing children's fitness levels (Gallahue, 1976).

There are several causes for the poor physical condition of our young children. First the urban/suburban environment often deprives children of fences to walk along and balance on, trees to climb, hills to roll down and large open spaces in which to play ball and run freely. Children who have not integrated the movement skills involved in the above activities need to acquire them sequentially in an educational setting during the early preschool years (Casebeer, Note 2). Children's facination for watching television has helped create a sedentary society for children. They are not getting enough physical activity in the form of free play and use of playground equipment. Even those children who participate in free play and have adequate open space available may not develop skills in all movement areas. Many children tend to stay with one free time activity until they gain a feeling of competency and success, while neglecting development in other areas. Active participation in <u>all</u> movement areas by children is essential to their development during these early childhood years.

It is essential for all children to have a good self-image. A positive self-concept is important in their overall development (Erikson, 1963). Movement experiences offer an important approach by which a positive self-concept can be fostered.

Children benefit from a feeling of <u>self</u>-satisfaction through achievement, in addition to benefiting from the positive feelings of others. Physical activities are valued highly by most children as well as by many adults. A child who does these activities well, will not only feel good about his own abilities, but will be praised by others also.

Movement education is of primary importance in the development of a good self-image (Casebeer, 1978). Children should have fun, be successful and feel challenged at the appropriate level by actively engaging in success-oriented activities. Movement experiences play an important role in how children perceive themselves, how they relate to their

4

peers and how they utilize their free time. "The development of a positive self-concept is too important to be left
to chance and we must do all that we can to assure its
proper development" (Gallahue, 1976, p. 125).

While involved in learning to move, children are
simultaneously involved in moving to learn, using their
bodies to gain knowledge about themselves and the world
around them. In order for learning to take place there
needs to be sensory information transmitted to the brain.
Once this information reaches the brain it is interpreted
and given meaning in light of previous information and
called perception.

There is a relationship between how children move and
how they learn. This concept is termed perceptual-motor
because it appears that how children perceive their surroundings, how they learn, and how they move, are related
and interdependent. Since maximum development of perceptual
abilities takes place between the ages of approximately 3½
to 7 years of age, the preschool is in the exciting position
to provide children with a strong base on which to build
future academic learning (Casebeer Note 2).

Movement activities are important not only for their
own sake, but for the contribution which they make toward
readiness skills which result from both maturation and
learning. A large part of readiness is motor learning.
Additionally, movement activities strengthen all three

<u>modalities</u> with which children learn: visual, auditory & tactual/ kinesthetic. Children need to be able to function effectively in all modalities because each learning style will be needed in various learning situations (Casebeer, 1981). The senses need to be strengthened so that the children will be able to switch modalities at appropriate times and learn in various ways: visually when reading a book, auditorily when listening to the teacher and tactually/kinesthetically when touching or manipulating tools or doing school projects.

Many theorists and educators agree that children's learning begins with movement and that their future <u>cognitive</u> success is greatly enhanced by full use of their senses and motor skills (Casebeer, 1976; Gallahue, 1976; Godfrey and Kephart, 1969; Piaget, 1952; Skinner, 1979; Spache, 1982). In other words, movement and thinking are interdependent.

One of the earliest investigators to come to the conclusion that all higher forms of learning are based on early motor experiences was <u>Jean Piaget</u>. Piaget believes that children eventually transfer physical actions into mental actions. Children learn about the physical world and the nature of objects by acting on these objects and by observing what happens as a result of their actions. They develop concepts of spatial relationships, movement efficiency, sequencing skills, perceptions of sizes, shapes, and timing which are all necessary for successful experiences in cognitive activities such as mathematics, science, language, reading and spelling.

Newell Kephart, a leading authority in the field of sensory education, believes that children need a great amount of experimentation in order to develop a perceptual-motor match (the matching of visual information with kinesthetic information) which is necessary in writing, reading, spelling, math and hand-eye tasks.

Children benefit from the language requirements of movement education. Their language skills can be enhanced by increasing their vocabulary as they learn the names of body parts, opposites and verbs for action. Additionally, children's language skills can be enhanced by increasing their ability to follow directions, sequencing a series of events and being 'teacher' (Casebeer, 1978). Cassell (1979) and Spache (1982) believe that listening skills of preschool children are improved by their ability to remember and respond to the rhythm of speech sounds. Spache (1982) states that reading (the discrimination of written language) is based fundamentally on the body, hand and eye experiences of children. Up-down and left-right discriminations are first learned in the muscles. Gradually children learn to translate the muscular cues of distance, size, direction-ality and shape into visual cues. The written component of language is an outgrowth of movement ability. Children must first be able to control their large arm muscles before being able to manipulate and coordinate the small hand and finger muscles. Readiness for writing also requires appropriate starting and stopping of an activity, and the rhythmic movement of hands and fingers (Skinner, 1979). Kephart (1960) would add other readiness requirements for writing: the ability to sit up, to hold one's head erect, to locate a beginning point for copying and to sequence. All of these skills are an outgrowth of movement experiences.

Movement education for preschool children is important in developing their physical potential, their self-esteem and their thinking skills. It is an important aspect of readiness for academic achievement in science, math and language. Let us make movement education an important part of the preschool curriculum!

THE PROGRAM

LEARNING TO MOVE, MOVING TO LEARN

Goals and Principles of
Movement Education

The goals of movement education for preschool children are: developing full use of all the children's senses, helping children develop good movement skills, enhancing children's positive self-image, developing children's cognitive skills and strengthening the children's three modes of learning.

To achieve these goals, movement education needs to be child-centered rather than teacher-centered. Because 50 percent of a child's potential for learning is developed by age 5, it is essential that effective child-centered movement education programs be available for preschool aged children (Van Oteghen & Jacobson, 1981).

In order to insure a child-centered program, movement education needs to incorporate the following principles:

1. Assessment and evaluation of the developmental level of movement skills of each child. A movement skills assessment checklist, as well as the directions for its administration and evaluation are included to determine each child's skill levels in order to provide movement experiences appropriate to his present stage of development.*

---

*In the interest of clarity "his" throughout the book refers to the individual preschool boy or girl. "Her" refers to the individual preschool teacher who is usually a woman.

2. Exploration of the many movements of which the child is capable. The child should be encouraged to try out all the possible muscular responses of which his body and imagination are capable.

3. Presentation of movement experiences which are appropriate to the child's present stage of development. For experiences to be successful and meaningful, they must be tailored to fit the child and his needs, not the needs of the teacher. Activities should begin where a child is, as shown by the assessment checklist, not where he should be on the developmental scale. Note: For special education students & IEPs see page i.

4. Presentation of skills sequentially with basic skills presented before more complex ones. A task should be simple enough to be grasped by a child within a reasonable time, indicating that learning has taken place.

5. Provision for variety and repetition. Each child needs a wide variety of developmentally appropriate movement experiences which will enable him to overcome any motor deficiency. Repetition, the opportunity for plenty of practice, is necessary for improved skill development.

6. Insuring the children's enjoyment of and success with the activities. Full and active participation by the children will help them to have fun. Children need to be busy doing movement activities, not waiting in long lines for their turn. Keep the sessions short, as the preschool child's attention span is limited. Providing positive encouragement will also add enjoyment to the activities. Deserved praise makes children feel good about themselves which adds pleasure to the activities. Many preschools use themes such as animals, transportation and seasons in planning the daily activities. Movement activities can be chosen and adapted according to these themes, which will make the activities even more fun, as well as adding to the child's understanding of these topics by unifying all aspects of the child's learning. Participating in movement activities which are multi-sensory, multicultural and non-sexist help children develop to their full potential! (Refer to pg. i)

Regardless of ability, all children need to be assured of movement success, which can best be fostered by using all of the child-centered principles which have previously been discussed.

The Teacher of Movement Activities

The quality and success of movement education is dependent upon the teachers. The positive growth and development of the children are affected by their teachers' knowledge, traits and characteristics. For teachers untrained in this area of education, practice and study will allow success in structuring movement experiences with the proper degree of guidance. The following is a list of desirable qualities for teachers of movement activities:

1. Know <u>each child</u> as a person as well as by assessment <u>of movement</u> skills. A child from a bicultural background <u>may</u> have difficulty with the <u>terminology</u> rather than the movement skills.

2. Have a real love for children and sincere interest in the <u>development of all aspects</u> of their potential: <u>physical</u>, <u>affective</u> and <u>cognitive</u>.

3. Possess <u>knowledge</u> and <u>understanding</u> of the growth and development of children.

4. Encourage <u>experimentation</u>, <u>exploration</u> and <u>creativity</u> by asking questions which require thought and by being respectful of (valuing) unusual ideas and original movement solutions of problem solving questions. <u>Never crush anyone's ideas</u>.

5. Say "do" instead of "don't." <u>Lead from the positive</u>, what the child can do (instead of saying, "Don't run," say "You need to walk.")

6. <u>Observe, analyze, offer suggestions</u>, assist only when needed and then observe some more.

7. Praise children for their positive actions, such as "I really liked the way you did that. Can you jump another way?"

8. Give children choices. This fosters success and self-esteem.

9. Remember that children learn by doing. More action and less talking is needed!

10. Choose both movement exploration activities as well as specific skill activities for each movement skill area.

11. Plan ahead. Know what your purposes are. Choose activities which can be individualized and allow for many developmental levels. Write your procedure on the weekly activity schedule (Appendix C). Assemble needed materials. Be ready and enjoy!

12. Record your observations for each child on the back of the student record sheet. This will allow you and others to plan for further activities.

13. Take small groups of children (two to six, depending on the activity) with similar skill levels for experiencing activities together. Children learn from each other. At times one child may need to work alone.

14. Be enthusiastic. Enjoy what you are doing. Choose or adapt activities which you find interesting as well as appropriate for the child's needs. When you have fun exploring movement with the children, spontaneity and eagerness result. An activity can be used in more than one skill area depending upon the emphasis given by the teacher.

Assessment

An assessment of each child needs to be done before he participates in movement activities. This will ensure that the activities are appropriate to his developmental level. This assessment can be repeated any time during the year as needed or desired. Follow the instructions which are entitled: "Instructions and Evaluation for the Movement Skills Assessment Checklist."

Movement Skill Areas: An Overview

After being evaluated, each child engages in developmentally appropriate activities first from Skill Area I, then from II, III, IV, V and VI. This cycle is repeated using other appropriate activities, providing a spiral effect. It is important to remember that most activities contribute to more than one aspect or skill area of movement, so that even though the emphasis is on one skill such as locomotion, balance and body parts are also being learned as well. Although rhythm and timing are an important aspect of all skill areas, they are placed at the end so that they can be included with movement education or used separately in a music curriculum.

Motor Skill Area I: Body Awareness

. Body parts--knowledge of what the body parts are and what they do

. Differentiation--control of separate body parts

. Coordination--control of both sides of body as well as upper and lower body parts

. Relaxation--control of relaxing separate body parts and whole body

Motor Skill Area II: Balance

. Static balance--balance while standing still. Develops
   first.

. Dynamic balance--balance while moving

. Object balance--balancing an object

Motor Skill Area III: Locomotion

. Locomotion activities--require use of space, time and
   energy: Rolling, Crawling, Creeping, Walking, Running,
   Leaping, Jumping, Hopping, Galloping, Skipping, Animal
   Walks, Climbing, Agility and Flexibility

Motor Skill Area IV: Spatial Relationships

. Laterality--"map of inner space"

. Directionality--"map of outer space"

. Personal space--amount needed varies with individual

. Common space--shared by the group

. Motor planning--involves space and time--learning a
   movement sequence: listening to instructions,
   attending to each detail & keeping the total sequence
   in mind.

Motor Skill Area V: Manipulation

. Manipulation--movement patterns which primarily
   involve or focus on manipulation, including contact,
   receipt and propulsion of an object. Included are:
   Throwing, Catching, Rolling, Kicking, Bouncing and
   Striking.

Motor Skill Area VI: Rhythm and Timing

May be used in the movement education program or separately
with music activities.

. Inner rhythm--develops first
. External rhythm--responding to outside rhythm and
   stimulus
. Flow of body movement/dance--depends on coordination

Early childhood education has the opportunity and responsibility to ensure that children maximize their physical, affective and cognitive development by providing them with many and varied movement experiences appropriate to their stage of development as determined from assessment or evaluation of their movement skills. Movement education truly plays an integral part in children's total growth and development. Let's help them <u>learn to move and move to learn</u>!!!

 Instructions and Evaluation for the
Movement Skills Assessment
Checklist

Each child needs to be assesed before participating in any movement activities in order to determine his developmental level in each skill area. This will ensure that the movement activities will be appropriate for him. The child may be reassessed any time during the year as needed or desired. Record the results on the student record sheet.

Read through the Instructions and Evaluation and assemble the materials listed at the end. Set up the activities and practice until the activities go smoothly.

Plan to complete the whole evaluation at one session and at a time when the child is in good health. The evaluator should check the child to be sure there are no physical factors to restrict his movement such as an injury, inadequate or ill-fitting shoes or clothing that binds.   If he wears glasses he should keep them on.   The evaluator can stand, sit, or move about freely as necessary to be in the best position to make the required observations.   Refer to page 11, # 1 when assessing children from a bicultural home.

The child should be greeted warmly and be allowed to become interested in the activity.   The focus should be on making it a game for the child rather than on a testing situation; however, BE ALERT FOR CHILD ABUSE SIGNS!! Refer to current literature on this important subject!

Keep the Student Record Sheets Alphabetized in a three-ring binder along with the Weekly Activity Plans- for easy access by all people concerned. This is especially important in a team teaching situation!

ASSESSMENT FOR 3, 4 & 5 YEAR OLDS: (See page 20 for assessment
                                        of 2, 6 & 7 year olds)

I.   BODY AWARENESS: IDENTIFYING BODY PARTS   SHOULD NOT BE DEMONSTRATED (Based on sequencing from Brigance, 1978)

Purpose: Evaluation of knowledge of body parts

Procedure: With child facing you, ask child to touch body part on command.   Place N for each body part missed.

3 year old:

feet	hair	hands
ears	head	legs
arms	thumbs	neck
stomach	chest	back
knees		

4 year old:
above list plus the following:
heels   elbows   shoulders

5 year olds:
above list plus the following:
ankles   hips   waist

Evaluation: If a child makes three or more errors in identification, is slow or has to "feel around" to find the body parts, mark N at the top of the whole section.

SECTIONS II-VI SHOULD BE DEMONSTRATED IF NEEDED
(Bicultural child: refer to page 11, #1)

II. BALANCE

Purpose: Evaluation of child's ability to maintain equilibrium.

Procedure:

A. Child stands on one foot and balances for a count of 2 seconds (3 year old) or 5 seconds (4 & 5 year old). Repeat task on other foot. Arms out at sides, OK.

B. Child walks heel to toe 6 feet on a taped line on the floor (3 year old) or balance beam (4 & 5 year old) for 6 feet with eyes on "focus card" placed at eye level on wall. Using arms for balance is OK.

Evaluation: If child shows difficulty balancing or with excessive postural adjustments, mark N. Note any problem.

III. LOCOMOTION

Purpose: Evaluation of child's gross-motor coordination and motor control--essential for the basic body movements of locomotion.

Procedure:

A. Child walks forward in a straight line with cross pattern movements to a goal about 15 feet away. (Left foot and right arm move ahead, then right foot and left arm move ahead.) This may be best observed as child walks naturally coming into room.

B. Child places both feet together and jumps in place inside 2 foot hoop without losing balance or stopping between jumps. (1 jump for 3 year olds, 3 continuous jumps for 4 year olds & 5 continuous jumps for 5 year olds). Count for child.

Evaluation: If child appears awkward, lacks coordination, appears rigid, mark N. Note any problem.

IV. SPATIAL RELATIONSHIPS

Purpose: Evaluation of child's ability to per-
              ceive and respond to directional body
              positions, and plan for movement
              sequence.

Procedure:
         A.   Ask child to stand facing you. Examiner
              assumes a position which child is to
              mirror. Do not say what you are doing.
              (One hand in air, one hand on waist.)

         B.   Ask child to watch examiner demonstrate
              a sequence. Do not say what you are
              doing. Child is to repeat the sequence
              2 times for 3 year olds, 3 times for 4
              year olds: (Stomp one foot, clap
              hands.)   5 year olds repeat 3 times:
                        (Jump & turn around.)
Evaluation: If child has difficulty in mirroring
              examiner, is slow in execution, forgets
              or perseverates movement, mark N. Note
              any problem.

V.   MANIPULATION

Purpose: Evaluation of child's ability to orga-
              nize his own body, measure and structure
              space around him, and to throw, track
              and intercept a moving object.

Procedure:
         A.   Place 2 foot hoop target in an upright
              position 1 to 1½ feet from wall. Tape
              an X on floor 6 feet from hoop. Child
              stands on X, picks up bean bags from
              floor and then throws them through the
              hoop. Accuracy: 3 out of 6 times (3 years)
              3 out of 4 times (4 years) & 3 out 4 times
              at 10 feet away (5 years).

         B.   Teacher stands 6 feet away from child &
              throws ball underhanded to child. Catches
              8" or 10" ball, 3 out of 4 times (3 year old),
              6" ball, 3 out of 4 times (4 year old) ,
              6" ball, 3 out of 4 times, 10 feet away
              (5 year old).

Evaluation: If a child makes 2 or more errors in cont-
              trol, coordination, or accuracy, mark N.
              Note any problem.

VI. RHYTHM AND TIMING

Purpose: Evaluation of child's inner rhythm and ability to sustain rhythmic movement. (Child coordinates inner & external rhythm -5 yr)

Procedure:

A. Examiner asks child to march around room like a soldier or like being in a parade until told to stop. (10 seconds). 3 & 4 year olds. Same to drum beat-5 yr. olds.

B. Sitting cross-legged, examiner demonstrates the pattern of lap, clap (with 2 hands, slap knees then clap hands together) and asks child to do pattern until told to stop. (10 seconds). 4 & 5 year olds only do this activity.

Evaluation: If child has difficulty sustaining a rhythmic pattern for 10 seconds, mark N. Note any problem.

VII. PLAYGROUND EQUIPMENT

Purpose: Evaluation of child's participating in climbing, jumping and landing, hanging, swinging, balance, coordination, spatial awareness, cooperation and safety awareness.

Procedure: As child uses playground, he discovers activities, makes choices, and uses equipment alone and with others.

Evaluation: Teacher observes child's choices, behavior, general ability and safety when using equipment and playing with others. If child needs a small group experience on equipment, mark N. Specify area(s) needing help.

MATERIALS NEEDED FOR ASSESSMENT

Wide masking tape . . . 6' length (3 year olds)
Balance beam . . . . . 6"x2"x6" (4 year), 6'x2"x4" (5,6 & 7 year)
Wooden block . . . . 12"x12"x2" (7 year olds)
Focus card. . . . . Picture to look at while balancing (3-7 yrs)
Hoop & stand . . . . 2' opening (3,4 & 5 year olds)
Hoop on floor. . . . 2' opening (3,4 & 5 year olds)
Bean bags . . . . . 6 (3 year olds), 4 (4 & 5 year olds)
Playground ball . . . 8-10" (3 year olds), 6" (4,5 & 6 year olds)
Tennis ball . . . . (7 year olds)
Record/tape & drum . . (5, 6 & 7 year olds)
Student Record Sheets . . Alphabetized in class notebook (3-7 yr. olds)

ASSESSMENT FOR 2 YEAR OLDS:

Assess the fundamental movement abilities of young 2 year old children by observing each child as he or she participates in basic, planned movement activities as well as during free play on the playground. Note any difficulty or any unsafe area. To evaluate older 2 year old children use the assessment for 3 year olds.

ASSESSMENT FOR 6 & 7 YEAR OLDS: (Refer to pages 16-19 for Purpose & Evaluation)

   I. BODY AWARENESS: NAMING/MOVING BODY PARTS (Should not be demonstrated)
      With child facing adult, instruct 6 year old to name body parts which adult points to on self (body parts listed on page 21A).
      Instruct 7 year old to move body parts on command: "Wiggle your feet." "Clap your hands." "Bend your elbows." "Shrug your shoulders." etc.

Sections II-VI should be demonstrated if needed (bicultural child: page 11 #)
  II. BALANCE
     A. 6 year old stands on floor & raises up on tiptoes & balances for 10 seconds. Arms out at sides OK.
       7 year old--same as above except stands on wooden block.
     B. Child walks forward then backward on 6' balance beam with eyes on focus card (6 & 7 year olds).

 III. LOCOMOTION
     A. 6 year old gallops for 4 gallops with one foot leading then switches feet.
       7 year old skips for 8 skips.
     B. Child hops 4 hops on one foot, hops 4 hops on other foot. Repeats sequence 2 more times, hopping with rhythmical alteration (6 & 7 year olds).

  IV. SPATIAL RELATIONSHIPS
     A. Touch child's right hand & say "This is your right hand." Child responds to the following verbal commands: "Raise your right hand." "Turn around to your right in a circle." "Put your right foot forward." (6 & 7 yr olds)
     B. Child repeats demonstrated sequence 3 times : Hop 2 times on one foot, then make 3 slides with other foot leading (6 & 7 year olds).

   V. MANIPULATION (Accuracy: 3 out of 4 times for A & B)
     A. 6 year old throws bean bag into the air & claps once before catching it.
       7 year old throws bean bag into the air & turns around before catching it.
     B. 6 year old catches 6" ball thrown by adult standing 8' away. Catches it with fingers & hands.
       7 year old catches tennis ball bounded by adult standing 8' away. Catches it with fingers & hands. (Ball bounces only once each time.)

  VI. RHYTHM & TIMING
     A. Play a rhythm record or tape with fast & slow tempos. Child is to move in time to the music by walking & jumping to the tempos (6 & 7 yr olds).
     B. Child listens to first set of drum beats (performed by adult), then claps an echo--4 sequences. Continue with second set of beats (6 & 7 yr olds).
      #1 Heavy 1, Soft 1-2   #2 Fast 1-2-3-4, Slow 1-2

 VII. PLAYGROUND EQUIPMENT
     Follow procedure located on page 19 # VI.

STUDENT RECORD SHEET
(3, 4 & 5 YEAR OLDS)
MOVEMENT SKILLS ASSESSMENT CHECKLIST

Student's Name_____ Birthdate_____

Marking: A=Above Average   Fall Date_____ Spring Date_____
          S=Satisfactory   Teacher_____   Teacher_____
          N=Needs Improvement

I.   BODY AWARENESS--Identifying Body Parts   Fall___ Spring___
     N=3 errors for 3, 4 & 5 year olds

3 year olds:	Fall	Spring			Fall	Spring
feet				chest		
hair				back		
hands				knees		
ears				4 year olds:		
head				heels		
legs				elbows		
arms				shoulders		
thumbs				5 year olds:		
neck				ankles		
stomach				hips		
				waist		

II. Balance
     A. Balance on one foot for a count of 2 seconds (3 year olds) or
                                    5 seconds (4 & 5 year olds)

Right foot		
Left foot		

     B. Balance line (3 year old) or beam (4 & 5 year olds)

Walks 6 feet looking at focus card (heel to toe)		

III. Locomotion

A. Walks forward 15 feet in cross pattern		
B. Jumps in place, 1 jump (3 year) or 3 jumps (4 year)		

                                        or 5 jumps (5 year)

IV. Spatial Relationships

     A. Child mirrors teacher

One hand in air, other on waist		

     B. Child repeats demonstrated sequence:

Stomp one foot, clap hands--2 times (3 year old), 3 times (4 year old); Jump & turn around-- 3 times		

                                        (5 year old)

V.   Manipulation

     A. Throws bean bag through hoop:

3 out of 6 times (3 year old--6 feet), 3 out of 4 times (4 year old--6 feet), 3 out of 4 times		

                                        (5 year old--10 feet)

     B. Catches ball:

8 or 10 inch ball--3 out of 4 times (3 year old)-6' 6 inch ball--3 out of 4 times (4 year old)-6' 6 inch ball--3 out of 4 times (5 year old)-10'		

22

Student's Name_____

Movement Skills Checklist continued (3, 4 & 5 year olds)

		Fall	Spring
VI.	Rhythm and Timing		
A.	Child marches around room, 10 sec.(3&4) w/ drum (5)		
B.	Demonstrates lap/clap pattern, 10 sec. (4,5 only)		
VII.	Playground Equipment		
	Child uses playground constructively and safely		
	Child uses playground with others		

Notes on child throughout year:

21A

STUDENT RECORD SHEET
(6 AND 7 YEAR OLDS)
MOVEMENT SKILLS ASSESSMENT CHECKLIST

Student's Name_____ Birthdate_____

Marking: A=Above Average   Fall Date_____   Spring Date_____
          S=Satisfactory   Teacher_____   Teacher_____
          N=Needs Improvement

I.   BODY AWARENESS--Naming/Moving Body Parts   Fall___ Spring___

3 year olds:	Fall	Spring		4 year olds:	Fall	Spring
feet				heels		
hair				elbows		
hands				shoulders		
ears				5 year olds:		
head				ankles		
legs				hips		
arms				waist		
thumbs				6-7 year olds:		
neck				chin		
stomach				toes		
chest				wrists		
back						
knees						

N= 3 errors for 6 & 7 year olds

II. Balance

     A. Balance on tiptoes 10 seconds:

On floor (6 yr olds), on wooden block (7 yr olds)		

     B. Balance beam: walks 6' with eyes on focus card

Walks forward then backward (6 & 7 year olds)		

III. Locomotion

A. Gallops 4 x's ea foot (6 yr), skips 8 x's (7 yr)		
B. Hops 4 x's each foot -3 sequences/rhythmically (6,7)		

IV. Spatial Relationships

     A. Child responds to directional tasks: Raise right hand,

turn to rt. in circle, put rt. foot forward(6,7yrs)		

     B. Child repeats demonstrated sequence 3 times:

Hop 2 times on one foot, make 3 slides with other foot leading (6 & 7 year olds)		

V.   Manipulation

     Child:
     A. Throws bean bag into air and

Claps hands 1x before catching bag (6 year olds)		
Turns around before catching bag (7 year olds)		

     B. Catches ball thrown by adult 8' away:

6" ball with fingers & hands 3 out of 4 x's (6 yrs)		
Bounced tennis ball w/ " & fing. 3 out of 4 (7 yrs)		

22A

Student's Name_____

Movement Skills Checklist continued (6 & 7 year olds)

		Fall	Spring
VI.	Rhythm and Timing		
	A. Child moves in time to tempo of music-fast/slow (6,7)		
	B. Demonstrates rhythmic patterns-heavy/soft, fast/slow -4 sequences (6,7 yrs)		
VII.	Playground Equipment		
	Child uses playground constructively and safely		
	Child uses playground with others		

Notes on child throughout year:

Skill Area I
Body Awareness

Body awareness refers to a child's concept of his body. The preschool child is continually exploring the movement potential of his body by gaining information about his body parts, what those parts can do, and how to make them move. Body awareness should not be confused with "self-image", which is the child's psychological concept of himself as a person based on personal worth and successful achievement.

Body Parts and Differentiation

Being able to identify and locate his body parts and distinguish between the two sides of the body are vitally important to each child. He must be able to discern one part of his body from another (differentiation) as well as know how all the parts move.

Body awareness is basic for the development of movement skills. Through guided participation in movement activities each child can explore and discover how his body is capable of moving.

Body Parts and Differentiation Activities

* Body Exploration

    . Encourage the children to look at and explore themselves. Attract their attention to their own hands, feet, arms, legs, head, etc. To do this, it may be necessary to stimulate the part for a child by tapping, rubbing, or stroking.

. Have the children touch their body parts to their surroundings: ask them to touch their heads to the floor, hands to the wall, knees to the floor, heads to tables or desks, backs to the wall, noses to the chalkboard, ears to chairs, fingers to bulletin board, stomachs to the floor, elbows to a door.

. Have the children touch body parts not only on themselves, but on dolls, Teddy bears & pictures. This activity can be used to introduce the topic: <u>prevention of child abuse/ child abduction</u>. Use current literature for the appropriate concepts at the children's developmental level.

. Teacher stands and gestures in different positions for children to mirror.

Examples:

Legs spread, 1 arm up, other down
Feet together, 1 arm at waist, other forward
Kneel, 1 hand on knee, other straight out,
   level with shoulder
Create a variety of positions for children to
   imitate.

Body image pictures may be purchased from educational supply houses, or a teacher may draw stick figures with different body positions.

Children must copy exactly as if they were looking into a mirror. Let other children serve as statues for their peers to copy.

. Tell the children to mirror you in the movement of a specific body part (in the beginning always identify the part): "Wave your hand." "Nod your head." "Close your eyes." "Open your mouth." "Stick out your tongue." "Wiggle your tongue." Use only a few each session; continue with many different parts: bend elbows, clap hands, twist neck, wiggle toes, shrug shoulders, bend knees, stamp feet, wiggle nose.

Four year olds: do the same activity as above, but do not demonstrate. Ask children to close their eyes.

. Following the leader:
Have one child be the
leader, followed by the
other children. While
walking, the leader calls
out a body part. The
children touch that body
part while continuning to
walk, (ears, neck, shoulders, nose, stomach, knee,
head, ankles, elbows, leg,
back, arms).

The leader should be changed **often**.

Arm <u>positions</u> and <u>movements</u> may be practiced in
the same way: one arm up, other arm up, both arms
up, both arms extended, both arms swinging.

. Children imitate repetitive rhythmic movement made
by the teacher.

Clicking sound with tongue.
Hands bend back and forth at wrist.
Elbows bend in and out from the body.
Shoulders shrug while standing.
One shoulder shrug
Hands slap on thighs.
One foot stomp. Alternate feet.
Head nod.
Hands beat on table. Be creative.
Children chant, da, da, da. Be creative. Change
   the rhythmic pattern and also the emphasis.

* Body Outlining

Have the child lie face up
on a large sheet of paper.
Outline his body with a crayon.
The child may then add other
body parts, such as ears, eyes,
mouth, nose, fingers, or
clothes to the outline.

* Verbal/Auditory Activities

. Using verbal commands, not demonstration, tell the children to:

Touch your knee to the floor.
Touch your hands to the floor.
Can you make your elbows touch your knees?
Can you touch your hand to your wrist?
Stand so that your arms are touching your sides.
Can you make your nose touch the floor?
Touch your foot to your head.
Stand so that your heels are touching the wall.
Make your knee touch your chin.
Hold your ankles with your hands.

Other examples:

nose to knees	wrist to ankle
chin to chest	elbow to stomach
ear to shoulder	wrists to chin
hands to hips	wrist to wrist
elbows to knees	fingers to fingers
toes to nose	hands to back
wrists to neck	arm to leg
wrist to ear	finger to nose
elbow to leg	toes to toes
chin to wrist	fingers to toes
fingers to shoulders	

. On a sunny day, children stand outside and look at their shadows. Give these directions: (Casebeer, 1978, p.62)

Make your shadow tall.
Make your shadow short.
Make your shadow wide.
Make your shadow thin.
Make your shadow touch its head.

. Talk about the uses of the body parts and have the children supply the name:

I smell with my_____.   I see with my_____.
I hear with my_____.   I talk with my_____.
I eat with my_____.   I kick with my_____.
I jump with my_____.   I blink with my_____.
I wave with my_____.   I shrug with my_____.
I walk with my_____.   I clap with my_____.

$\longrightarrow$

```
I hop with my_____.    I nod with my_____.
I sniff with my_____.    I point with my_____.
I taste with my_____.    I kiss with my_____.
I stand on my_____.    I throw with my_____.
I kneel on my_____.    I wear a belt around
I fold my arms across         my _____.
   my _____.
```

. Teacher says "What do you call this?" "What is
  the name of this?" Teacher points to body part
  and child answers. For added interest, hand
  puppets may be used while the child tells the
  puppet the name of the body part...or the child
  and teacher can both have puppets.

. Have a collection of pictures of specific body
  parts and have the children identify them. Use
  feet, face, and body puzzles.

* Movement Exploration/Creative
  Movement Activities

. Egg roll: Place L'eggs on
  floor. Roll egg with part of
  the body.

  Examples are:
  nose, elbow, foot, head.

. Have children pretend to be colored balloons and
  blow themselves up by blowing into their thumbs.
  The children try to pass through geometric shapes
  set up on stands, using different body parts going
  through first. Each balloon can pop and be blown
  back up.

. Balls. (Nerf ball works well at first.)
  "Can you...?"

  ...roll it around your neck?
  ...roll it down to your chest to your waist?
  ...roll it around your waist one way and then back
     the other way?
  ...roll it down one leg going to your knee and on
     down to your foot?
                                            ⟶

...roll it around one foot and then around the
     other foot?
...roll it back up your other leg across your
     chest and up to your chin?
...roll it across your cheek and then your nose
     and up to your forehead?

* See Body Parts Activities listed under Rhythm &
   Timing (Section VI)

Coordination

Coordination is the harmonious functioning of the
muscles in a skilled movement pattern. This skilled movement may involve primarily foot-eye coordination (kicking a
ball), hand-eye coordination (throwing a ball at a target),
symmetrical coordination (integration of both sides of the
body (as in creeping), or overall coordination (swimming).

Good coordination is essential to successful performance in games, sports and dance. Of course, those movements which are more complex call for a greater degree of
coordination. Remember that in order to produce a well-
coordinated movement, the specific skills involved must be
practiced many times.

Children can develop greater movement efficiency by
practicing coordination skills involving the various body
parts.

The success of many future classroom activities depends
upon how well the child can make his eyes and hands work

together, as well as how well he can control his large muscles for sitting activities.

Coordination Activities

* Angels in the Snow (Skinner, 1979, p.9)

> Child lies flat on his back on the floor, arms at sides and feet together. It is important that he feels contact with the floor to increase his awareness of the position of his hands and feet at all times during the exercises.

> Have the child move his feet apart as far as he can--he should not bend his knees and must keep his heels on the floor. On returning to the starting position (at your request), have him bring his heels together with a snap.

> Now have him move his arms along the floor until they touch above his head. He should not bend his elbows, and he should keep his wrists and hands in contact with the floor.

> If he needs help to move arms and legs together or separately, help him only until he gets the "feel" of the movement.

>> Touch or stroke one arm. Say, "Move this arm." Touch or stroke his other arm, then each leg, saying each time, "Move this ____."

> Next, try it by pointing to an arm or leg without tactile reinforcement. Point to one arm and say, "Move this arm." Proceed as before without touching the limbs.

> Combine arm and leg movements now. Keep working with a child for no more than 3 minutes at a time until arm and leg movements are smooth and well coordinated. He should not show superfluous movement of those limbs not required for the

requested task. If he has difficulty making independent movements, hold down the limb that should not move while he moves the other limb.

* Coordination Activities

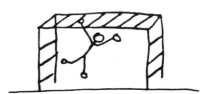

> Jog in place
> Jump in place
> Climb up and down steps
> Swing from bars
> Climb ladders
> Swing from rings
> Ride tricycle
> Jump in and out of hoops
> Run through tire patterns
> Climb through monkey bars

The use of any playground equipment that demands coordinated use of arms and legs is good for this skill.

* Scooter Board

Child can use scooter board to:

> Sit on and push with feet
> Lie on tummy and pull with arms or push with
>   feet

At first child should use board in a straight line, next go around two cones, and later, in an obstacle course.

* Bimanual Circles

Place a fixation point (an X) on the chalkboard at the nose level of the child. The child stands about 10 inches from the chalkboard. Holding a piece of chalk in each hand, he places the chalk in contact  with the board at about 1 inch from the fixation point. The child starts by moving hands upward,
→

making a circle pattern on the board with both hands simultaneously. The left hand is moving counterclockwise and the right hand clockwise. The child makes numerous circles with both hands, trying to improve on the contour of the form to make a perfect circle. These movements may be changed by having the child's left hand move clockwise and the right counterclockwise, or by having both hands move in the same direction.

* Creative Expression (Franz, Note 3)

. "See what you can do with just your fingers, hands, arms and different parts of the body. Now move every part of your body."

Make yourself round.
Make yourself very quiet and relaxed.
Wiggle like a worm.
Be an astronaut floating in space.
Be a balloon being inflated, let go, then popped.
Be an egg beater.
Gallop like a horse.
Be a washing machine.
Carry something very heavy on your head.
Be a cloud drifting in the sky.
Be a boat tossed on the waves.
Make yourself tall; ...small.
Slink like a cat.
Crawl like a snake.
Be a tin soldier.
Grow like a flower.
Walk on a tightrope.
Be a yo-yo.
Be a typewriter.
Be a top.
Be a monkey swinging from the trees.
Be a wind-up toy.
Walk like an elephant.
Walk like a spider.
Be popcorn being popped.
Be a nail being hammered into wood.

. The Seed Story (Franz, Note 3)
You are a seed buried in the ground.
You feel wet and warm under the ground.
The sun is shining very brightly.
You slowly begin to crack open the seed.

You are beginning to grow.
You are slowly growing up through the ground.
Your leaves start to open.
You are growing bigger, wider and taller.
The sun is covered
    by a huge rain
    cloud.
You are cold.
The wind begins to
    blow.
The rain begins to
    fall.
You are blown from
    side to side.
The rain is pounding you down to the ground.
The ground is muddy and wet.
You feel heavy and wet and tired.
Suddenly the rain stops and the wind stops.
The sun is bright again.
You slowly lift yourself from the ground.
You open your leaves to dry them in the sun.
You are warm again from the sun.
You feel strong, firm and tall.

. Body Play (Moving Story)
    Hot-Cold (Opposites) (Franz, Note 3)

You are in a cold room. There is no fire or heat.
You want a jacket. You look for one. You can't
find a coat. You are freezing.

You are in a warm room. The windows are closed
and locked. The heater is on. It cannot be
turned off. You are very warm and are sweating.
It is daytime. The sun will not stop shining.

Other opposites to use in your own body play:
    closed-open   slow-fast
    narrow-wide   over-under
    loud-quiet   up-down
    soft-hard   come-go
    limp-stiff   high-low
    move-freeze   forward-backward
    heavy-light

. Movement Phrases (Franz, Note 3)

    I don't know.   --shrug shoulders
    I'm so happy.   --squeeze self →

```
I love you.              --hug
Walk quietly.            --tiptoe
I want to hide.          --crouch
Help, this won't move.  --tug
He hit me!               --jerk away
```

. Emotions

Have the children move and express the emotions listed below. It is important for the teacher to act as a model to initiate movement.

angry	sad
happy	silly
sleepy	afraid
mad	helpless
lonely	glad
love	shyness
friendship	laughter
surprise	tears
hurt	

* See Coordination activities listed under Rhythm and Timing (Section VI).

Relaxation

It is important that all children learn to relax. Some children need guidance in making the transition from hard physical exercise to relaxation. Our society is characterized by an increase in stress and anxiety for children as well as adults. This is due to family and economic pressures, and also media coverage of tragedy and disaster.

Even though some stress is useful, indeed even helpful, the unrelieved, generalized stress that is pervasive in modern life is nothing but destructive to children. Children need to acquire skills that will enable them from time to time to pull back from the turmoil. (Cherry, 1981, pp. 3-4).

One function of movement education is to teach children what tension feels like, what to do to relax and ease the symptoms of stress, thus helping them to acquire lifelong relaxation techniques.

Tension relaxation activities involve body-part awareness, integration of thought and feeling, and an outlet for (and reduction of) anxiety. These activities are often helpful for children who are under normal daily pressures of life.

Relaxation Activities (Franz, Note 3)

* Tension Awareness and Letting Go (Isometrics)

Children find a space on the floor and lie down.

Tense your right leg as hard as you can. Hold it until you can't keep the tension, and then let it go.

In the following steps, tense, hold and let go as in the first step.

Tense the buttocks and hip area as hard as you can.
Tense your right arm as hard as you can and let go.
Tense your right shoulder as hard as you can, and let go.
Continue through facial muscles, left shoulder, left arm, hip and buttocks area again, and left leg.
Tense your entire body as hard as you can, and let go.

(Relaxing background music is helpful but not essential.)

* Arm-Breathing and Leg-Breathing (Franz, Note 3)

 . Children stand in space of their choice.

> Breathe in deeply. Exhale. Breathe in deeply, let the arms rise. Exhale and let the arms return to the sides.

 . You may use this same exercise from a position where the children lie on the floor. Instead of letting the breath take the arms into space, the breath takes the legs into space.

* S t r e t c h

> Stand up and s t r e t c h for the sky with your arms! Stretch! Now relax and be limp all over like a rag doll. Stretch your neck like a giraffe at the zoo. Kick your feet like a donkey. Wave your arms like a monkey. Roll your eyeballs in circles like a clown. Blink your eyes. Wiggle your eyebrows. Now curl up in a ball like a fluffy kitten.

* Relaxation

Breathing. Repeat each activity 5 times.

> Sit down or lie down. Take a deep breath. Hold it for a count of 5.
>
> Take another breath on top of the first one and hold it for a count of 5.

> Whoosh air out and stay limp.
>
> Flap hands vigorously for a count of 5. Let hands hang limp.
>
> Swing arms in a large circle for a count of 5. Let arms hang limp.
>
> Take a deep breath. Hold it for a count of 5.

Take another breath on top of the first one and hold it for a count of 5.

Whoosh air out. Remain quiet and limp for 1
minute. Do not move!

* Isometrics

All isometrics should be done until the muscles
tire, usually to a count of 10.

Tighten and release:

jaws	shoulders
forehead	neck
diaphragm	buttocks
knees	ankles
toes	elbows
wrists	fingers

* Yoga Breathing

Children sit tailor-fashion in a comfortable
space.

Breathe in deeply.
Exhale.
Breathe in deeply and let breath carry arms
    up.
Exhale and let the arms come to rest on the
    knees.

* Creative Movement

. Ice Cream Cone

Let's be ice cream cones on a sunny day.
What flavor of ice cream do you want to be?
    (Children choose a flavor.)
Now everyone stand tall and place arms over
    head in a circle to form an ice cream cone.
Our ice cream is cold, round and firm, but
    soon the sun comes out and it becomes
    hotter and hotter.
We begin to melt slowly. (Children slowly
    sink to the ground.)
It is hotter and we melt and melt.
Finally we are just a puddle on the ground.

. Snow Fun

Pretend to be a snowflake and float slowly
  through the air.
Now Mr. North Wind blows you quickly through
  the air.
Finally you fall on the ground.
Children come outside to play in the snow.
They take you and your snowflake friends
  and roll you in a ball.
The children make a snowman.
Now stand and pretend to be that snowman.
It's cold.
The snowman stands straight and tall.
The sun comes out.
It gets warm and the snowman begins to melt.
It gets hotter, and hotter, and the snowman
  gets smaller and smaller.
Finally, the snowman is a puddle of water.

. Can You Feel it?

Lie on the rug.
Be very, very still.
Now lay your hands on your chest.
SHHH!
Can you feel your heart beat?
Thump, thump, thump. Can you feel it?
Take a deep, deep breath.

Put your hands on your stomach and breathe,
  breathe, breathe.
Can you tell me what is happening to your
  hands?
Yes, they move up and down as you breathe,
  don't they?

Breathe in again. Take a deep breath, like
  this.
Can you hold your breath 'til I count to 5?
Now put your hands up to your mouth.
Open your mouth. Breathe in.
Now let your breath out through your mouth,
  like this.
Can you feel your breath on your hand?

Now close your mouth.
This time put your hand in front of your
  nose, like this.   →

Take another deep breath and let the air out
   through your nose.
Can you feel it?

Now just relax and breathe in and out, in and
   out, in and out...

. Rag Dolls

Talk to children and demonstrate after everyone is
seated on the rug.

        Let your head get all
           loose, like this.
        Now let your shoulders
           droop, then let your
           arms hang loose and
           floppy, then your body,
           then your legs.
        Are you all loose and
           floppy?
        Now close your eyes.
        SHHH!
        The rag doll is going to
           sleep.
        SHHH!

. Playing Possum

        (Talk quietly.) The opossum is a cute little
        furry animal that looks a little like a rat
        because he has a long, long tail. His face
        is white. He can go to sleep hanging upside-
        down by his tail. Sometimes he just pretends
        to be sleeping.

        Pretend you are all opossums and lie very,
        Very still, so no one will know you are here.
        Is everyone very, very still?
        I'll come around and move your arms or legs,
        and remember--you don't want me to know you
        are really awake!

. Kitty Cats

        (Speak slowly.) Lie on the rug and close your
        eyes. Pretend you are all little kitty cats,
        sound asleep. Do you know how cats can just

barely open their eyes, s l o w l y and
s t r e t c h?

> Can you stretch like a cat?
> Stretch way out!
> Now the kitty slowly closes his eyes and goes
>   to sleep again.
> Don't move.
> Keep your eyes closed and rest a minute.
> Can you think of something very nice?
>   ...like a birthday party, or running in the
>   park or wading in the water? What do you
>   like to do that's fun?

. Quiet Time   (Skinner, 1979,p.91)

(With children on rug, speak slowly and quietly.)

> I've just come in from playing
> As tired as I can be.
> I'll rest my legs
> And fold my hands.
> I'll close my eyes
> So I can't see.
>
> I will not move my body,
> I'll be like Raggedy Ann.
> My head won't move,
> My arms won't move,
> I'll just be still...
> Because I can.

On a warm day it's delightful to lie on the
     cool, green grass and watch the
          clouds and birds
               drift by.

. Oodles of Noodles
  (Franz, Note 3)

How would you feel
and look if you were
an uncooked noodle?
Show me how your
fingers would look, your arms, your whole body.

→

You're cooked now and ready to be served.
Show me how you move as you are lifted out of
the pot and plopped on a plate.

Oh! Oh! There's a fork under you. It's
lifting you up.

Ooops! You're slipping off...

Now the fork winds you round and round...

And suddenly you disappear because you've
been eaten up!!

* See Relaxation activities listed under Rhythm and
   Timing (Section VI).

Skill Area II

Balance

Balance, an important aspect of all movement, is the ability to maintain one's equilibrium in relation to the force of gravity by making minute alterations in one's body position.

Static balance is the ability to maintain one's equilibrium in a stationary position such as standing on one foot.

Dynamic balance is the ability to maintain one's equilibrium while the body is in motion, such as walking on a balance board.

Object balance is the ability to balance an object on one's body; carry one or more objects, such as bean bags on one's outstretched hand or carry a picture puzzle.

Good static balance is essential for success in dynamic balance, which in turn, is essential for balancing objects.

Developing good balance is very important for each child. It aids in acquiring smoothly coordinated movements, which allows the child to move with self-assurance--an important element in improving chances of success during playground and classroom activities (Lerch et al., 1974). When the child can move easily in a coordinated manner, his mind is freed to concentrate on other matters.

A "focus card" should be used for balancing activities. The child looks at this card (hung at eye level) while balancing. The focus card should be interesting to the

child and can be coordinated with the school theme, such as
cut-outs of a Valentine, pumpkin, zoo animal or airplane.

Static Balance Activities

* Stork Stand

What is a stork? (Explain if
  child does not know.)

Can you stand on one foot like
  a stork?
Can you stand on your other
  foot?
Stand on one foot and see if
  you can count to _____
  before you put your other
  foot down.

(Repeat using the other foot.)

Can you close your eyes and stand very still on
  one foot like a stork?

(Repeat using the other foot.)

2 & 3 year olds stand for 1 second.
4 & 5 year olds stand for 5 seconds.
6 & 7 year olds stand for 10 seconds.

* Balance Play   (Casebeer, 1978, p. 71)

One child is the sun.
One child is the rain.

Other children squat with heads down in designated
spaces. They are seeds under the ground. The
rain comes and sprinkles each seed. Heads raise
up. The sun comes again and shines on each seed.
Arms raise up. Rain comes again and sprinkles
each seed. Children slowly stand, keeping arms
raised.

*Freeze (or Statues)

. The children walk or sway to the rhythm of music.
  When the music stops, they must stop, or "freeze",
  and hold whatever position they are in until the
  music starts again.

. Children can also run, creep or do animal movements until they hear a musical signal (triangle,
  drum beat) then freeze.

. When asked to walk:
        on tiptoes
        on heels
        fast
        lightly
        forward
        heavy like an elephant
        with long steps
        backwards
        sideways
        freeze on one body part
        freeze balanced on 2 or 3 body parts

. When asked to run:
        like a horse
        in a straight line
        in a zigzag line

. When asked to hop:
        as high as they can
        take short hops
        take long hops
        on one foot

. When asked to jump:
        like a frog from one
           lilly pad to another
        over a small box

* Twister Game (by Milton Bradley)

    Teacher can be spinner or children can take turns.
    One or two children can play at a time.

* Balance Blocks

    Balance blocks can be cut to various sizes depend-
    ing upon the ability of the children: 12" x 2"
    x 12" Place these on a surface which is not
    slippery.

        Can you balance on both feet?
        Can you balance on one foot?
        Can you touch _____ (body part) while
            balancing?
        Can you balance _____ (high, low)?
        Can you balance with a partner?
        Can you find a new way to balance?

* Balance on Body Parts (Lerch et al., 1974, pgs. 101-102)

    Can you balance on four
    parts of your body?

    Can you balance on four different parts?
    See how long you can balance.

        -knees and hands
        -knees and elbows
        -feet and hands

    Can you balance on three body parts?
    What other three parts can you balance on?

        -2 knees and 1 hand
        -2 hands and 1 knee
        -1 foot and 2 hands
        -head and knees
        -head and feet (done
          on mat)
        -1 elbow and 2 knees

    Can you balance on two body parts?
    Can you balance on two different parts?
    What other two parts can you balance on?

        -feet
        -knees
        -1 hand and 1 foot (same
          and opposite side)
        -1 knee and 1 hand (same
          and opposite side)
        head and knee (on mat) →

Can you balance on one body part?
What other part can you balance on?
Can you think of another part?

-right foot
-left foot
-right knee
-left knee
-seat

Dynamic Balance Activities

* Scooter Board (Skinner, 1979, p. 15)

The scooter board is an excellent device for balancing because a child lies on his stomach with his body supported by his trunk; his head, arms and legs are elevated. This is a basic postural pattern from which he should be able to pivot.

. When the prone position is mastered on the scooter board, have the child try the same activities in a sitting position, legs brought up toward his chest.

Observe whether the child exhibits protective extension of hands or feet to protect himself as he approaches a wall or obstacle.

NOTE: Children must be closely supervised when using the scooter board. Children must never stand on boards. Strict rules must be set up before allowing children to use the boards. ALWAYS store the boards with wheels up.

. Self-propulsion: child pushes himself with hands; goes from one place to another; follows a curved "road" (parallel lines made with chalk or tape).

Blast off: child pushes off with hands or feet against a wall for speed. →

Obstacle course: child goes through and under objects designated by teacher.

Twirling around: spin on the scooter board, first in one direction and then the other.

Other activities:
    child holds onto a rope as the teacher pulls him.
    teacher holds ankles and pushes child.
    with two children on boards, they carry items back and forth to each other.

* Coordination Ladder (or "ladder" taped on floor with masking tape)

Ladder should be placed flat on the floor. The child walks <u>forward</u>, stepping in the spaces <u>between the rungs</u>.

Have the child walk <u>backward between the rungs</u>.

Have the child walk <u>forward</u> stepping <u>on the rungs</u>.

Have the child walk <u>backward</u> stepping <u>on the rungs</u>.

Ask him to <u>walk on all fours on the rungs</u> like a monkey.

After he has mastered these activities, encourage him to do them without watching his feet.

* Dancer

Children stand on tiptoes with arms out.
Lean trunk sideways and lower one arm while other arm goes up, maintaining tiptoe balance.
Slowly go upright and lean trunk other way and lower arm and raise other arm up, maintaining balance.

$\longrightarrow$

Slowly go upright again and down to standing
   position.
Repeat 3 times.

* Dramatic Interpretations

The children do dramatic interpretations of people
moving about as if they were:

very old	young
a witch	a majorette
a soldier	very angry
very sad	in a hurry
like a clown	afraid
worried	looking for something
hiding	climbing
walking in mud	digging
throwing	picking up something heavy
walking a dog	just smelled a skunk
dragging some- thing heavy	walking with a hurt leg

Strive for maintaining balance as children move in
different postures.

* Jack-in-the-Box   (Skinner, 1979, p. 18)

Have the children squat with their hands on their
heads--this is holding the lid down on the "box." To
build up suspense, say very quietly and slowly, "Jack
is hiding down in his box until someone opens the
lid." When the teacher says the word "lid", the
children spring up and jump with their legs apart.
After playing a few times, let the children take
turns being the leader.

* Walk the Rope

Children should walk barefooted, with
heads up looking at focus cards.

. Let's pretend your rope is a very
   narrow bridge. Can you walk all
   the way to the end without falling
   off?

   Remember to use your arms to help
   you balance.   →

Variations:
    Have the children walk heel to toe
    Have the children walk leading with one
      foot and sliding the other up.
    Same as above, but with other foot
      leading.

. Now let's pretend that the rope is a tightrope in
a circus. Can you walk the tightrope backwards?

. The rope is lying over a river now. See if you
can walk sideways on the rope without falling in.

    Have children walk sideways leading with
      other side.
    Same but cross one foot over the other.

* Using Playground Balls

    Child sits on ball and lifts one foot and tries to
      balance. Hands on floor.
    Child sits on ball and lifts both feet and tries
      to balance. Hands on floor.
    Repeat stunts with hands and arms held forward.
    Child lies on stomach on ball and tries to balance
      using hands only on floor.
    Child lies on stomach on ball and tries to balance
      without touching hands or feet on floor.

* Bridge Balance (dynamic and static)

    Build a bridge over a bean bag
      laid on floor by using four
      body parts touching the
      floor.
    Repeat using 3 body parts.
    Make a long, high, low, draw
      bridge.

* See Balance activities in Rhythm and Timing
(Section VI).

* Balance Board (also referred to as walking board or
balance beam) (Skinner, 1979)

Balance board activities are most effective when done
with bare feet. Extra time is needed for taking off

→

and putting on shoes. Make this part of the learning activity by stressing: (1) placement of putting socks in the shoes, and (2) sequencing: first, "Put on your socks." Next, "Put on your shoes." And last, "I'll help you tie your shoes if you need help."

For most 3 and 4 year olds a 2' x 6" wide by 6' long board is used.

For most 5 year olds a 2" x 4" wide by 6' long board is used (this is called a balance beam).

Many teachers and therapists agree that most children master a walking board more easily if they are left alone to figure out how to use it by themselves, without constant adult supervision.

The teacher must make certain that all children have the opportunity to practice. She must encourage and supervise the child who is hesitant or fearful.

Balancing is easier if the child's eyes focus on a specific target, or "focus" card, which can be tied in with the school themes: a picture of a train, a jack-o-lantern, or a spider.

Teacher may want to hold the child's hand and walk beside him or let the child put his hand on the teacher's arm as they walk.

. Most children will have no fear of the low walking boards and will need no preliminary activities. Others must be taken through the process step by step:

1. Have child first walk a chalk or tape line on the floor, heel-to-toe.
2. He should progress to a rope laid flat on the floor in a straight line.
3. When he has practiced doing this, place the walking board flat on the floor until he feels secure, then raise the board.

. Children should walk slowly across the balance board trying to maintain their balance and should not step off the board more than twice while moving from one end to the other. They should use both arms as a counterbalance. Movements should

→

be fairly smooth, not jerky, and their bodies should show no overt tenseness or rigidity.

. Encourage those children who master a forward heel-to-toe walk to try walking backward. They may look back to see where to place a foot, or they may search with their toes to locate the board behind them. Encourage them to do a smooth backward walk without having to look.

. Have the children walk the board sideways. Step, slide. Some of the older children may be able to do a cross-over step. Then they might try walking across the board, turn (half-turn) and return walking sideways. After that, they can try a full turn by walking across the board forward, turning, and return walking forward.

. Other activities are:
      Walk to the middle, turn around and walk back.
      Walk to the middle, turn around the other way and walk back.
      Walk to center, squat down or lower weight, stand up again, continue to end.
      Walk length of board touching heel of foot in front to toe of one behind.
      Tiptoe to end of board.
      Walk board with long stick or pole in both hands.
      Walk board with ball in both hands.
      Walk board with hands on top of head.
      Walk board with a weight in each hand.
      Walk board with a weight in one hand.
      Walk board with a weight in other hand.
      Walk board with a weight in both hands behind body.
      Walk board with arms out to sides.
      Walk board with one arm extended in front and one behind.
      Walk with opposite (other) arm extended in front, and other behind.

$\longrightarrow$

Walk board stepping over a series of bean
   bags spaced along board.
Walk board with textures taped to board (soft
   velvet, scratchy nylon net, bumpy bubble
   pack).

Object Balance

Be creative in devising object balance tasks. Use a
variety of materials and let the children explore
this type of balancing. The objects should have a
variety of weights, shapes, textures and properties.
Be certain that the children use only safe materials.

Children enjoy balancing:

sticks, balls, bean bags on
   various places on the body:
   chin, shoulder, head, knee,
   foot, wrist, elbow.
an object on an object: bean
   bag on a book, block on a
   block.
liquid in a container: water
   in a pitcher or cup.
two objects or more: 3
   blocks, several spoons on a
   tray.

Skill Area III

Locomotion

Through locomotion, a child is able to effectively explore the world around him by transporting his body from one location in external space to another, such as by walking or jumping. The child acquires locomotor skills in the following progression: rolling, crawling, creeping, walking, running, leaping, jumping and hopping. He can then combine these movements so that he can do animal walks, gallop and skip.   He can climb, hang by his hands and "walk" across playground ladders, developing his upper body strength.

The child who becomes fully aware and in control of his own locomotor movements develops a feeling of self-worth and self confidence essential to his behavior and future learning.

Rolling

Rolling is one of the most basic activities in body movement. Moreover, it is extremely important in the stimulation of the vestibular system, development of balance and coordination (Skinner, 1979).

Rolling Activities

* Log Roll

    . Have the children
      lie on a rug or mat
      on their backs and
      roll their heads to
      the right and to the
           ⟶

left, touching their ears to the mat. Now have them extend their arms above their heads with their legs straight out. Roll over, head first, then arms, followed by the hips and legs.

Ideally, children should not lift up their heads or buttocks while rolling. However, the knees may be bent a little.

. Have children roll from their backs to their stomachs and return to starting positions. Then have them roll from their stomachs to their backs and return to starting positions.

. Let children roll in the grass and watch the world go 'round. If there is an incline on which they can roll down, this is especially good for them.

Crawling   (Skinner, 1979, p. 67)

In the crawling position, the children lie down on their stomachs with heads and shoulders raised by supporting the weight of those areas on the elbows. Have them crawl forward, stomachs touching the floor, by moving the elbows and hips. Most of the body movement comes from pulling with the arms and pushing (swimminglike movements) of the legs.

First have the children move in a homolateral pattern (moving arm and leg on the same side together). Then have them crawl in a cross-pattern manner (moving the right arm and left leg together, and the left arm and right leg together). To begin, have them crawl forward and backward, then through an obstacle course. The children can be worms, snakes, caterpillars, snails--anything that crawls on its stomach.

Crawling Activities   Record: "Boa Constrictor",(Peter,Paul,
                          and Mommy, 1785,Peter, Paul, and Mary)
* Worms (Tune: "Frere Jacques")
      Worms are crawling, worms are crawling,
      All around, all around,
      Digging little tunnels, digging little tunnels,
      In the ground, in the ground.

      When it's raining, when it's raining,
      Out you come, wiggle worms,
      Crawling in the puddles, crawling in the puddles,
      How you squirm, wiggle worms.

* The Happy Snake (Tune: "Mary Had a Little Lamb")
      The snake is crawl-
        ing all around,
      All around, all
        around,
      The snake is
        crawling all
        around,
      To see what he can
        see.

      And as he crawls he makes no sound,
      Makes no sound, makes no sound,
      And as he crawls he makes no sound
      As happy as can be.

* Little Snails
      The little snails are so-o-o slow,
      They crawl along the ground,
      And as they crawl they make no sound.
      The little snails are so-o-o slow.

* The Seal (Tune: "Farmer in the Dell")
      The little black furry seal--
      Around the pool he crawls,
      Back and forth with a happy squeal,
      Then splash! in the water he falls!

Creeping   (Skinner, 1979, p. 68)

    The children get up from the crawling position onto

their hands and knees. Knees are lifted for each step, but

the feet drag along the floor. Knees should move forward in parallel lines with hands pointing forward, palms flat on the floor.

Homolateral creeping consists of the hand and knee of the same side moving together--right hand with right knee, left hand with left knee.

Cross-pattern creeping is the ultimate goal: the hand on one side and the knee on the opposite side move forward together. If a child cannot creep in the desired cross-lateral pattern, direct him to look at the forward hand as it reaches out. His neck and head should turn as he looks at the forward hand. The constantly changing head position provides continuously changing sensory-motor clues for the eyes. With practice and direction, a child can be taught to move from a less mature (homolateral) to a more refined (cross-lateral) creeping stage.

Have the children creep forward, backward and sideways. Add various textures to enhance tactile stimulation.

<u>Creeping Activities</u>

* Wooden Geometric Shapes   (Skinner, 1979, p.69)

> Have the children creep through geometric shapes. Call out the shape you wish each child to creep through--circle, square, triangle, etc. Ask each child to show you how he can creep through the red shape, the green one, the blue one. Have the children tell you which shape or color they are going to creep through: circle, square, triangle, red, green or blue.

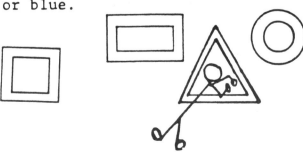

* Roly, Poly Caterpillar (Tune: "Row, Row, Row Your
    Boat")

    Roly, poly caterpillar,
    In a corner crept.
    He settled down and closed his eyes,
    And there he safely slept.

* Worm Through the Apple

    Children stand close together in a line with feet
    about 12" apart. One child is the worm who
    wiggles (creeps) through hole made between legs.

* Little Indians (Chant) +

    The Indians are creeping.
    Shhh! Shhh!
    They do not make a sound,
    As their knees touch the ground.
    The Indians are creeping.
    Shhhhhh!

* The Alligator (Tune: "The Bear Went Over the
    Mountain") +

    The alligator is creeping, the alligator is
        creeping,
    The alligator is creeping down by his pond.
    Down by his pond, down by his pond.
    The alligator is creeping, the alligator is
        creeping,
    The alligator is creeping, down by his pond.

* Busy Spiders (Tune: "The Farmer in the Dell") +

    They creep along the walls,
    They creep along the floor,
    And after they spin their webs,
    The spiders creep some more.

* Mr. Turtle (Tune: "Skip to My Lou") +

    Mr. Turtle, in your shell,
    You creep along so very well,
    Up and down the hills you go,
    But Mr. Turtle, you're so slow!

 + Record: "Lion" (Rhythm Time, B301, Lucille Wood)

Walking
====

Walking requires both balance and coordination, with the arms and legs alternating and swinging freely. Just walking can be boring for the children while walking to music is much more stimulating and fun. Be sure to choose music in which the beat is neither too fast nor too slow for the types of walking you wish to do (Skinner, 1979).

Walking Activities
----

* Walking Patterns

There are many different walking patterns for the children to follow while walking to music:

walk forward
walk fast
walk with hands
  behind back
walk with feet
  turned out
walk with tiny
  steps
walk on tiptoes
walk on tiptoes
  with hands
  over heads
walk forward and
  backward with
  knees up high
  (slow march)

walk backward
walk slow
walk with hands
  on hips
walk with feet
  turned in
walk with giant
  steps
walk on heels
walk like robots
  or mechanical
  toys (knees
  stiff)
walk with feet
  turned out

* Movement Exploration

.   Can you walk in this direction without bumping
      into anyone else?
    Can you walk backward in this direction without
      bumping into anyone else?
    Can you change direction when I say forward or
      backward?
    Can you walk forward very quickly? (On toes)
    Show me how you walk very high.

Show me how low you can walk.
Show me how you change levels while walking
  forward. (High to low and back again.)
Can you keep your hands low while walking at a
  high level?
Show me how you keep your hands high while walking
  at a low level.
Can you change levels, while walking when I clap
  my hands?
Can you change direction, while walking, when I
  clap my hands?
Show me how you walk when you are happy?
  ...angry? ...frightened? ...tired? ...sad?
Can you walk a circle pattern while moving in this
  direction? ... **in a square?**

. Suggestions for guiding walking movements:
      How high, how low?
      What direction? ...backward? ...forward?
        ...sidewards? ... upward? ...downward?
        back-and-forth?
      Can you go under? ...over? ...below?
        ...beneath?
      How big?   ...little? ...soft? ...hard?
        ...strong? ...weak? ...smooth? ...jerky?
        ...shaky? ...swingy? ...loose? ...tight?
        ...heavy?
      How fast? ...slow (not so fast)?

* Walk the Shape

    Place various wooden geometric shapes on the floor
    or make shapes with tape

    Hold up a shape made of paper and ask the child to
    find the same shape on the floor. Name the shape.
    Name the color of the shape.

    Child walks (skips, tiptoes, heel-to-toe) around
    the shape.

    Continue with all shapes.

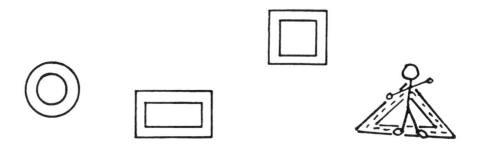

* Hoop Walk   (Lerch et al., 1974, p. 120)

Several hoops are placed in some pattern on the
floor. Children are in a line in front of the
hoops.

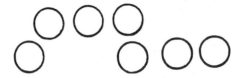

Can you walk forward stepping into each hoop
   without touching it?
Can you do the same thing walking backward?
Can you walk sideways without touching the
   hoops?

* Pathfinder   (Lerch et al., 1974 p. 119)

Curved, zigzag and straight paths are drawn or
taped on the floor. Children are asked to move
around the floor until they come to a path. The
teacher gives verbal instructions as they move.

Pretend that you are an Indian (or animal)
walking through the woods. When you come to
a path, see if you can walk forward on it
without falling off. Walk forward on each
path you find. Keep moving around the room
looking for paths.

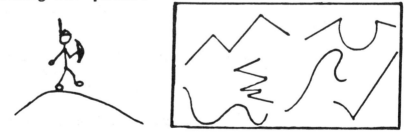

Keep moving on the paths. Now see if you can
walk backwards on the paths you find.

Can you walk sideways without falling off?

* Tightrope Walk

First draw a line with chalk or put down a 6 foot
strip of masking tape. Have the children walk the
⟶

line heel-to-toe. Progress to a rope on the floor. Tell the children to walk the "tightrope" like a circus performer. This should be done in bare feet for tactile/kinesthetic feedback.

* Sidestep (Sliding) (Skinner, 1979, p. 71)

Children step to the side with the right foot and slide left foot over to meet the right foot, bending knees slightly. This should be practiced going both to the right and to the left.

Have several children move around a circle using the sidestep, moving slowly, then moving quickly, first to the right, then to the left. (Use the terms one foot, other foot, or mark right foot with a red dot and left foot with a blue dot.)

Cross-over step: Children cross left foot over right foot, bringing right foot behind left foot, crossing left foot over the right again. Now have them try it by crossing the right foot over the left. This is a much more difficult task than the sidestep.

* Skating (Skinner, 1979, p. 72)

Children participating in this sliding activity place each foot in a
small-size shoe box. Children should
slide their feet along the floor as
though they are skating. Try it with
music; a waltz is best to encourage
an easy, sliding movement. Arrange a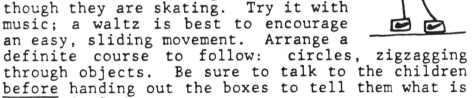
definite course to follow: circles, zigzagging
through objects. Be sure to talk to the children
before handing out the boxes to tell them what is
expected of them.

* Toy Soldiers (Skinner, 1979, p. 73)

This is a cross-pattern walk and especially good for those children who show poor walking patterns. Teach them to point at the forward foot with the opposite hand. That is, as a child steps out with the left foot, he points to it with the index finger of his right hand; when he steps forward with the right foot, he points with the left finger. Encourage the children to turn their heads and bodies toward the foot to which they are pointing (upper part of the body should be turned slightly at the waist). The eye and hand should be coordinated as in cross-pattern creeping. A few minutes at each session should be devoted to this until the children show good coordination. Colored dots can be placed on opposite hands and feet; red dots on right hand and left foot and blue dots on other hand and foot.

* Follow the Heart

    Place masking tape on floor in shape of a large heart. Move on tape in the following ways:

        Walk along tape.
        Walk with one foot on tape and the other
          inside heart.
        Walk with one foot on tape and the other
          outside heart.
        Walk inside heart.
        Walk outside heart.

* Walking in the Snow

    Act out motions while adult says verse:

        Let's go walking in the snow,
        Walking, walking on tiptoe.
        Lift our one foot way up high,
        Next the other to keep it dry.
        All around the yard we skip.
        We watch our step, or we will slip.

Running

    Running is a locomotor progression of walking. Running requires more balance than walking because both feet leave the ground during each stride. (Skinner, 1979, p. 79)

Running Activities

* Basic Running Activities   (Skinner, 1979, p. 73)

    Run forward.
    Run backward.
    Run with hands over heads, on hips, behind backs.
    Run "in place" (standing in place moving legs up
        and down)--begin at a slow pace and gradually
        build up to hard run, then slow down to original
        slow pace while counting rhythmically.
    Run with streamers. (Cut crepe paper streamers
        2 inches wide of different colors; have children
        grasp one end of paper which trails out when
        they run.)

* Movement Exploration

    Who can run to the wall and back?   Show me.
    Can you run high? Low?
    Can you run straight? Crooked?
    Can you run light? Heavy?
    Can you run and keep your heels from touching
        the floor?
    Can you lift your knees when you run?
    Can you point your toes when you run?
    Can you run among your friends without
        touching anyone?
    Run and stop on signal.
    See how quickly you can stop
        running when the signal is given.
    Run and change direction on
        signal.
    Take as few running steps as
        possible to get from one point to
        another.
    Run taking as many steps as
        possible.
    Run backwards.
    Run as quietly as possible,
    Run changing the speed at different signals.
    Show me what you can do with your arms while you
        are running.

Leaping

    Leaping is the next locomotor progression of running--a

long stride--although it can be done from a standing position as well. Give the children opportunities to leap from a standing position and to leap in a running stride. Some of the activities used for running and for hopping may be used, substituting leaping (Skinner, 1979, p. 77)

Leaping Activities

* Jack Be Nimble (Skinner, 1979)

Glue a toilet tissue cardboard roll onto a flat, square piece of cardboard (the base) for a candle-stick. A paper towel roll may be used for the older, more capable children. Even though Jack "jumped" over the candlestick, a leap is the more natural movement, and even most pictures in nursery rhyme books show leaping, not jumping. Improvise with other props as the children advance.

> Jack be nimble, Jack be quick,
> Jack jumped over the candlestick.
>
> Jack be nimble, a leap he
>   took,
> Jack jumped over this
>   little book.
>
> Jack be nimble, quick as
>   a fox,
> Jack, jumped over this
>   cardboard box.
>   (small one)
>
> Jack be nimble, quick I hope,
> Jack jumped over this long white rope.
>
> Jack be nimble, light as air,
> Jack jumped over this little chair.
>   (use toy chair)

Jumping and Hopping

Jumping is when both feet leave the ground together. To jump, a child squats with arms forward, swings arms back and springs up. The knees should bend on landing. He should land without losing his balance. If a child has trouble getting his feet off the floor to jump, stand in front of him. As he begins to jump, help him to carry through by lifting him by the waist. When he gets the "feel" of the entire movement, he should be able to carry through by himself (Skinner, 1979).

Hopping is a one-foot takeoff similar to jumping. Jumping and hopping are also excellent for developing rhythmic balance.

Jumping and Hopping Activities

* Jumping

    Jump in the following ways:
    As high as possible
    As far as possible
    Backward, forward, sideway
    Jump and try to turn around in the air
    Jump and land as quietly as possible
    Jump being frogs
    Jump being jumping jacks

* Over the River

    Place two pieces of string parallel on floor about one foot apart. Explain that this is the river to cross to get to Grandma's house for Thanksgiving dinner. Jump across the river without falling into the "water." Place strings farther and farther apart. Children can sing the song as one child jumps. At other times of the year, this can be called "Jump the Brook."

* Rope Jump/Hop

    Place a long jump rope on the floor and direct the
    children to:

        Jump from side to
         side with both feet
        Hop on one foot from
          side to side with
          alternating feet
        Bunny-hop from one
        side to the other
        side.

* Hoop Jumping/Hopping

    Place 3 to 5 hoops on floor in a line or scattered
    pattern.

        Child should jump with both feet in each
          hoop.
        Can repeat going backward.
        Repeat with hopping--use one foot, then
          other.

* Ladder Hopping

    Make a likeness of a 7 foot ladder on the floor
    with masking tape. Have the children:

        Hop on one foot in each space, then using the
          other foot.
        Jump with both feet.
        Repeat going backward.

* The Grasshopper

    Have a grasshopper or picture of a grasshopper to
    show.

        Have you ever seen a grasshopper? Show
          how a grasshopper hops up and down.
        Pretend the grasshopper has only one leg.
          How would he jump?
        Can you jump across the floor like a
          grasshopper?

* Rabbit Hop/Jump

Have children squat with their knees together
between their arms. Their hands should be flat on
the floor, and their weight should be put on their
hands. The hands should move first, reaching
forward, with the knees and feet following. Both
feet should leave the floor together in a jumping
action. Have them hop across the room or a grassy
area.

* Kangaroo Jump

Children stand with feet together, bending elbows
and letting hands dangle limply about chest
height. They then get into squatting positions,
spring up, and hop forward with both feet at once.
They then return to squatting position.

* Jumping Boxes   (Lerch et al., 1974, p. 105)

Several boxes (of different colors) should be
scattered around floor.

    Stand behind a box. Can you step up on the
        box, jump into the air and land in a
        balanced position?
    Go on to the next box and
        do the same thing.

With younger children boxes
may be placed in front of the
mats. Children may be asked
to move to the boxes using
different locomotor movements:
Hop, slide, skip, run, walk,
on all fours, crab walk, bear
walk, elephant walk.

    Jump in a different way off each box you
        come to.
    Can you jump and turn in the air?
    Can you stretch your arms up high as you
        jump?
    Can you spread your feet apart and bring them
        together before you land?
    Children can jump into a hoop placed in front
        of the box.

Galloping   (Skinner, 1979, p. 81)

Galloping is a combined leap and hop--one foot takes off in a leap, then the other hops. Body weight remains on the same side. The children should be taught to lead with either foot. Eventually they should be able to switch from one side to the other without difficulty. This ability is prerequisite to skipping, which will be learned around the age of 5 to 6 years

Galloping Activities

* Galloping Horses (Tune: "Skip to My Lou)--Galloping + Ponies or Reindeer

    Galloping, galloping, galloping GO!
    Galloping, galloping, galloping GO!
    Galloping, galloping, galloping GO!
    Galloping, galloping, galloping WHOA!

* I'm a Cowboy (Cowgirl) (Tune: "Ten Little Indians") +

    Gid-di-up, Gid-di-up, I'm a cowboy!
    Gid-di-up, Gid-di-up, I'm a cowboy!
    Gid-di-up, Gid-di-up, I'm a cowboy!
    Riding on a pony!

    (Second verse: I'm a cowgirl)
 + Record: "Galloping Horses" and "Ponies"
            (Rhythm Time #2, B303, Lucille Wood)
Animal Walks

* Creature Movement

  . Worm Wiggle (good for crawling)

        Lie on stomach. Hold arms at side. Try to move body forward without using hands or elbows.

. Grasshopper Leap

Squat with fingers touching floor. Leap
upward and forward. Return to squatting
position. Continue to leap across room.

. Spider Walk

Bend over so that fingers and feet are
touching the floor. Lift one leg and arm
very high in front of body and stretch. Take
a very long step. Repeat with opposite leg
and arm.

. Caterpillar Creep

Stretch out on floor. Bring back part of
body up to meet front half. Then stretch
front part of body out again.

. Butterfly Flutter

Move arms up and down as if flying. Fly
around room.

. Flight of Bumblebee

Move arms in figure eight motion. Pretend to
fly around room while making a buzzing sound.

* Cat Spring

Get into squat position with hands in front of
body on floor. Reach out forward with hands,
placing them on the floor. Jump out on feet to
meet hands, returning to original starting
position.
Cues: reach and jump.

* Angry Cat

Assume a creeping position. Arch
the back like an angry cat pulling
the head down toward the trunk.
Then straighten the neck and let
the spine slowly sink back to
resting position. Then creep.

* Swimming Fish

    Pretend to be a fish swimming in water.

        What type of fish do you want to be? Lie down on your stomach with your arms close to your side. Wiggle your body and try to move. Describe what you see in your underwater world. Act out the following verse:

            There is so much activity beneath the
              sea.
            Act out the creature you want to be.
            The crab crawls, the fish wiggles,
            The octopus swims, the jellyfish
              jiggles.

        Now you are the fish again. How would you rest when you are tired? How would you eat? Where would you hide if there was danger?

* Gorilla Walk

    Bend over and clasp ankles with hands. Walk that way allowing only a slight bend to knees.

* Alligator Creep

    Move forward on abdomen, using arms and legs to move body (cross-lateral creep).

* Frog Jump

    Get in squat position, placing hands on floor between knees. Jump up and forward, landing back down in beginning position.

* Rabbit Jump

    Get in squat position and put hands upon head to make ears. Jump forward, always returning to squat position.

* Seal Walk

    Get into push-up position with body weight on
    straightened arms and the top of feet. Keeping
    the body straight, walk hands forward, dragging
    the feet.

* Crab Walk

    Get into crab position (stomach facing up),
    holding hips up with feet heading forward. Walk
    on hands and feet using cross-lateral pattern.

* Elephant Walk

    Bend forward at waist, keeping head down. Join
    arms together in front of body to make a trunk.
    Walk forward slowly, swaying trunk back and forth.

* Bear Walk

    Bend body over and touch the ground with hands.
    Travel forward slowly on hands and feet, using the
    unilateral pattern (right hand and right foot
    together; left hand and left foot together).

* Dog Run

    The hands are placed on the floor; the arms and
    legs should be slightly bent. The child runs
    forward on hands and feet, in a cross-lateral
    fashion.

* Lame Dog Walk

    Get into cat spring position, then lift one leg
    straight back off the ground. Arms reach forward
    as before and foot hops forward to meet hands.
    Cues: reach and hop.

* Going to the Zoo

    Child must choose an animal to imitate as his
    means of getting to the zoo.
    $\longrightarrow$

> We're going to the zoo. How is Diana going
> to get there?
> I'm going to fly like a bird (says Diana).
> ...hop like a frog, waddle like a duck,
> swim like a fish, crawl like a snake.

Agility and Flexibility

Agility is the ability to change the direction of one's body rapidly and accurately while moving from one place to another as rapidly as possible.

Flexibility is the ability to bend one's body easily and refers to the range of motions of the various body joints. The following activities will enhance children's development of agile and flexible movements.

Agility and Flexibility Activities

* Who Can Do This?
  Have the children placed so they are not touching one another and have enough space in which to move. One of the best ways to motivate is to precede each exercise with the words, "Who can do this?"

  -Who can do this? Stand on your tiptoes. Up! Now down! Now up! Down, up, down! Good for you, Cindy! John can do it! Look at Paul and Gayle! Up, down, up, down, faster, faster! (Keep talking.)

  -Who can do this? Bounce on your feet. Bounce with your feet together, like this. Now bounce with your feet apart. (Keep praising individual children, being certain to mention all names.) ⟶

-Who can do this? <u>Twist your tummy</u> (twist at waist). Twist with your arms straight out in front of you, and twist back and forth, back and forth. Swing those arms!

-Who can do this? <u>Put your hands on your hips</u>, like this. Now bend way forward. Now up. Now bend way back. Now up! Forward, up, backward, up. Forward, up, backward, up.

-Who can do this? Make your <u>head roll 'round</u> and 'round <u>and 'round</u>.

-Hold your <u>arms</u> way out to your sides, like this and make them <u>go around</u> and around in big circles.

-Drop your <u>arms</u> and <u>swing</u> them--whoosh--forward and backward, forward, backward.

-<u>Squat down</u> verrrrrrry slowly while I count to five. Go back up again, slowly, slowly, while I count to five again.

-<u>Jump and reach up high!</u> Bend those knees! Up you go! Jump! Reach for the sky. Jump! High! High! How high can you jump, Tommy? Look at Ann! I didn't know Sharon could jump so high!

-Make up <u>other</u> Who Can Do This <u>challenges</u> with the following movements:

bend	sink	stretch	sway
twist	push	swing	pull
wiggle	bounce	shake	rise
fold in	stretch out		

* The Bell

Stand with feet apart, arms relaxed at sides. Bend forward, keeping knees still and swing the upper torso and arms in a sideways motion.

* Stretch

    Children sit, legs spread and flat. Lean forward,
    grasp one ankle with hand and pull the head down
    toward the leg. Change legs.

* Ride a Horse

    Have the children squat and extend their hands,
    pretending to hold the reins of a horse. They
    should flex their knees and bounce up and down.

* Inch Worms

    Have the children stand tall, then put their hands
    on the floor or ground in front of their feet,
    keeping their knees stiff. They should "walk"
    their hands away from their feet as far out in
    front as possible. Then keeping their knees
    straight, they "walk" their feet up to meet their
    hands. Repeat.

* Bear in the Winter/Spring

        Let's pretend to be a bear.
        Walk like a bear by bending knees slightly,
          bend back and touch hands to the floor.
        It begins to get cold so the bear finds a
          cave.
        He curls up and goes to sleep.
        Warmer weather comes and the bear wakes up
          slowly from his long winter's nap and
          stretches.

* Halloween Walk

    Line up on one side of room. Cross in following
    ways: (Use nonsexist approach.)

        Fly like a bat.
        Gallop like a cowgirl...cowboy.
        Hop like a bunny.
        Roll like a pumpkin.
        Dance like a princess...prince.
        Creep like a cat.
        Walk like a skeleton.
        Float like a ghost.

* Make-Believe World

    Individually, or in small groups, children make believe that they are other people, animals, plants, machines, weather conditions, etc.

       -Pretend you are soldiers. How do soldiers march?

       -You are the pilot of a big jet airplane. Can you show me some of the things you would do? Can you take off in your plane? Can you land it?

       -Let's pretend you are monkeys in the jungle. Show me how monkeys move. (Same with other animals like elephants, tigers, dogs, snakes, ducks.)

       -A spell has been cast and you have all been changed into witches. Show me how you would act. How do witches fly?

       -Pretend you are a train. Can you go forward? Can you go backward? How does a train move going up a big, steep mountain? How does it move coming down the mountain?

       -Have you ever ridden in a big truck? Pretend you are driving the truck. How would you move? Can you drive the truck on a winding road? How does a truck sound?

       -Let's make believe you are the leaves on a big tree. How do the leaves move when the wind blows? What happens to leaves that have been blown down? How do they move?

* Let's Pretend (Bernice Wells Carlson as found in Franz, Note 3)

    Before you read a verse, ask a child how he would make the motion which the verse suggests, such as "How do you ride a pony?" Ask him how the pony would fall down. Emphasize the fact that the children must stop at the end of each verse.

       Oh let's pretend! Yes, let's pretend
       That we are something new.
       Let's pretend we're lots of things
       And see what we can do.

→

David is a cowboy   (Rosa)
Riding up a hill
Until his pony stumbles   (her)
And David takes a spill.   (Rosa)

Jennie is an autumn leaf   (Jose)
She twirls and twirls around   (he)
She twists and turns and twirls again (he)
And tumbles to the ground.

Kathy is a candle straight
Too bad! She got too hot
She's bending almost double
Something like a knot.

Kevin is an airplane   (Juanita)
Flying high and grand
Until he sees an airport   (she)
Where he has to land.   (she)

Sally is a firefly   (Hans)
Flitting in the night
Until the morning comes
And she puts out her light.   (he)(his)

Ken is a snowman   (Kim)(snowwoman)
Who smiles and looks around
Until the sun smiles back at him (her)
And melts him to the ground.   (her)

What else can you pretend?   (Primary children
What do other people do?   can create their
If you will act it out,   own actions and
I'll try to do it too.   rhyme (poem)

The ideas for body imagery are endless. Look at
animals, insects, machines, the environment, to
see how they move. Experience different textures
to see how they feel. Use a variety of vocabulary
words. Have the children choose which "something
new" they wish to act out.
-Note: Use a non-sexist approach.

* "Let's Pretend" was adaped for this publication by
  June Gustafson Munro.

* The Parachute (Skinner, 1979, Pgs. 87-88)
        (Good for Manipulation also.)
     If available, a parachute can be used to improve
     strength and flexibility of arm and shoulder
     muscles. Although children enjoy parachute
     activities, the novelty wears off if it is
     overused. Keep activities simple and brief. The
     parachute can be used both indoors and outdoors.

     To begin an activity, spread the parachute out on
     the floor. Explain that everyone must work
     together as a team in order for the activity to be
     really fun. Have the children line up evenly
     around the parachute and grasp the edge with both
     hands. The children can grasp it easily if the
     parachute is rolled toward the center 3 or 4
     times.

     To "inflate" the parachute, have the children hold
     it at waist level, then count and hold the edge
     against the floor or ground. Count: 1,2,3, UP!
     Everyone must rise and stretch their arms high
     above their heads to get an inflation. This will
     have to be done several times in order for all the
     preschoolers to understand what is expected of
     them and to work better as a team.

. The Bubble (or Balloon)
        Begin as above. When the children have
        lifted the parachute over their heads, have
        them take two steps forward to allow the
        chute to make a big "bubble" or "balloon."

. The Mushroom
        This is the same activity as the Bubble
        except that after inflation, the children
        squat and pull the edges down to the floor or
        ground to close the bottom of the chute. The
        center of the canopy will descend to the
        floor with a mushrooming effect.   →

. The Tent

After inflating the chute, the children walk
two or three steps to the center, pull the
chute down over their shoulders, and sit down
inside the "tent" as it descends.   Count:
"One, two, three, IN!"

. Fly Away

When the chute is inflated, tell the children
to "Let go!" After they release the canopy,
it will float gracefully to the floor.

. Ocean Waves

Have the children hold the chute at waist
level.   On the command, "Make waves", they
alternately lower and raise their hands
causing the chute to billow up and down.
Larger waves are made if done in unison, but
a rhythm must be set for them: "Up, down,
up, down, up, down."

Variations:

Place a few light-weight balls in the
center of the chute; the children move
the balls around.

. Merry-Go-Round

Have the children walk around in a circle
while holding the edges of the chute.   On
command, they stop and walk in the opposite
direction.

Skipping (For 5 & 6 year olds)   (Skinner, 1979, p. 82)

Skipping requires the prerequisite of accomplished galloping-
being able to switch from one side to the other easily.
A skip is a step then a hop on the same foot with the arms
swinging freely in a cross-lateral pattern (in opposition).   It
requires a shift in body weight from side to side as well as good
balance and timing.
Breaking the movements down into a pattern/sequence will help
First take a step, then hop with the same leg, then switch weight,
step, then hop with the other leg.   Establish a rhythm: step, hop,
step, hop, step, hop, step, hop.
Refer to the index, under skipping, for suggested activities.
Skipping can be used with most rhythm and circle games (see games)
as well as with locomotion activities. Traditional songs, such as
"Skip To My Lou" and "Pop Goes The Weasel", can be made into fun
skipping games. The children can make up their own rules, there-
by developing their creativity and leadership skills.
Note: Refer to page 106, cooperative games/full participation.

SKILL AREA IV

SPATIAL RELATIONSHIPS: LATERALITY
DIRECTIONALITY, COMMON SPACE,
PERSONAL SPACE AND MOTOR PLANNING

Spatial relationships refer to a child's awareness of his own body symmetry, the spatial characteristics of an object, and his ability to perceive the position of two or more objects or people in relation to himself and in relation to each other.

A child first learns about space through tactile sensations (touching objects). He learns spatial ideas before he learns the words to describe the actions, such as "up", "down", "in front of" and "behind." He learns to apply these concepts and perceive spatial relationships of objects outside and beyond himself. He can then move himself and objects within that space and, finally, visualize what an object would look like if it were moved into a different position (Skinner, 1979).

Through many movement experiences involving space and direction, the child will be able to execute a sequence of movements in the correct detail and right order (motor planning), thus becoming more confident of his ability to manage his body in a variety of daily situations.

<u>Laterality (Map of Inner Space)</u> (Skinner, 1979)

Laterality refers to the inner sense of one's own symmetry. The preschool child is in the process of slowly developing an inner awareness for the difference between the two sides of the body. Until this is established, he may lack feeling for the midline of his body, have difficulty planning space, show poor balance in many activities, and probably will not establish a dominant side. The child who has not yet achieved a sense of laterality will "mirror" the action of the one side of his body with the same (or similar) action on the other side.

The identity of "right" and "left" may not come until the child reaches the age of about 5½. The words "right" and "left" are only terms, and knowing this is not in itself laterality. Dominance grows out of stabilized laterality.

Moving through space requires both sides of the body to act as a team, and in this sense, we speak of bilaterality. Effective movement requires coordination between the two sides of the body. For example, when throwing a ball, one side of the body does the throwing and the other provides balance and follow-through.

The order in which most children learn <u>directional/positional</u> concepts (Brigance, 1978) is: ⟶

Age 3	Age 4	Age 5	Age 6
up/down	bottom/top	low/high	front/back
out/in	over/under	inside/outside	right/left
	far/near	beginning/end	right/left of others
	go/stop	off/on	to/from
		closed/open	here/there
		above/below	
		forward/backward	
		away from/toward	
		center/corner	
		straight/crooked	
		through/around	
		going/coming	

Sequence of directional/positional concepts (also laterality)
(Brigance, 1978)

Laterality Activities

* Direct the children to move in specific directions, using one body part, then the other, then both or all.

    Put one arm on top of your head.
    Put your other arm on top of your head.
    Put both arms on top of your head.
    Put one foot over your head.
    Put your other foot over your head.
    Put both feet over your head.
    Put one hand under your bottom.
    Put your other hand under your bottom.
    Put both hands under your bottom.
    Put one knee high in the air.
    Put your other knee high in the air.
    Put both knees high in the air.

* See Activities for Body Parts in Section I.

* See Activities for Balancing in Section II.

* Bean Bag

    Each child holds a ball, bean bag or other easy to hold object. Directions are given to hold the object in various positions. (See Brigance list above for appropriate concepts relating to the body.)

        Examples:
            over your head
            under your chin
            behind your back
            between your knees

Directionality (Map of External Space)

    Directionality is an outgrowth of laterality and refers to the external sense of objects in the environment in relationship to one's body. The table is on your right. The roof is over your head. The dog is walking in front of you. All of these concepts are in relation to one's body or another object. The idea of directionality also takes form in the terms right, left, front, back, over, under, inside of, beside, on top of, and many, many more. Because directional concepts are understood in relationship to one's body or to another object, they are difficult concepts which the child learns with time and experience. He understands them before he speaks of them. (Refer to the top of page 81 .)

    <u>Form discrimination</u> refers to the ability to recognize differences in basic form: shape, straight & curved lines & size--essential for reading & writing. Size constancy, however develops more gradually as the child matures.

    When working with colors and shapes, remember that it is important to present one characteristic of an object at a time. Color precedes form. Sorting and matching colors comes before sorting and matching abstract forms. A child will learn that a circle is blue before he learns that it is round. After color perception is developed, colors can be used as cues to help in assimilating other qualities, such as shape. (Point to the blue rectangle, the green triangle.) Remember that a child will probably be able to follow the direction, "Point to the red one" before he can answer the question, "What color is this?" Or, "Point to the circle," before he can answer the question, "What shape is this?" (Skinner, 1979).

Directionality Activities

* Pointing

    . Direct the children to point: in front of them, in back of them, to the side of them, to the top and bottom of objects in the room.

         Point over the door   ...over your shoulder
         ...below the window   ...above a picture
         ...under a chair   ...over a wastebasket
         ...between 2 children

    . With eyes closed point to the door, window, wastebasket, floor, ceiling, cupboards, over your own head, at the teacher.

* Go

    Have the children place themselves in different positions in relation to objects in the room:

         Go in front of the chair.
         Go under the table.
         Go in the circle hoop.
         Go up the stairs.

* Magnet Movement

    Child will pretend to have a magnet in his finger, nose or elbow and is pulled to various positions:

         The magnet is pulling your elbow high.
         The magnet is pulling your elbow forward.
         The magnet is pulling your elbow over the
             box.

* Mirroring

    Children mirror the teacher's body positions or
    various body position cards. Refer to imitation
    Body Parts in Section I.

* Directional Course

    Set up a directional course which will require the
    child to go over, under, between and around
    certain obstacles (tables, chairs, cones, wands).

        Can you step over the first wand?
        Can you walk between the chairs?
        Can you walk around the chair?

* Can You Follow Directions?

    Equipment should be scattered around area so that
    the child can walk freely: 2 chairs, 1 mat, 1
    long rope, 1 short rope, 1 door, 1 ring (circle).

        Can you point up?
        Can you point down?
        Raise your right hand.
        Crawl under the chair.
        Can you stand in front of a chair?
        Stand behind a chair.
        Sit in a chair.
        Find a circle. Can you jump into the circle?

        Can you jump out of the circle?
        Lie down on the mat.
        Stand off the mat.
        Pick up the long rope.
        Find the short rope and pick it up.
        Can you place your feet above your head?
        Place your hand below your knees.
        Find the circle. Can you walk around the
          circle?
        Can you walk between the chairs?

* Wooden Geometric Shapes

    Creeping through geometric shapes is an excellent
    activity to promote the development of form
    discrimination and spatial awareness. Three
    shapes (circle, square and triangle), two each,

painted in colors make up a basic set for pre-school. The shapes can be used in an upright position with support stands or placed flat on the floor or ground for throwing bean bags or hopping/jumping activities as well as creeping.

Have the children creep through the shapes.
How many different shapes are there?
How many colors?
Can you creep through the circle?
Can you creep through the blue one?
What shape is the blue one?
Which one has 3 corners?

* **Exploring the Shapes**

Place various shapes around the room to allow the child to go under, over, around, through, and between them. These shapes may be made from cardboard, plywood or plastic tubes. Smaller shapes are also needed as cues.

Teacher holds up a shape and asks the child to find a similar shape.

Can you go over the shape? Under it? Around it? Through it?

The child is encouraged to explore the shape on his own.

Common Space (Shared by the Group)

Common space is that which is shared by two or more children. Some children by nature will require a great deal of personal space while other children will need very little (Casebeer, 1981). At circle time or gathering time, enough space should be allowed so that each child can have the amount of space around him which he needs. Overcrowding can cause behaviors such as pushing and should be avoided.

Some children need help in discovering that there is space between themselves and others.

Common Space Activities

* Bubbles

> Children will sit on floor finding their own space by putting arms out to feel their bubble.

* More Bubbles

> Children find their own space, and pretend to have bubbles in their hands. The bubbles can be blown, gathered in, pushed, bounced. Background music can be added.
>
> > Use imagination to set the mood and activity such as:
> > Children pretend to be stepping on bubblegum..
> > Children pretend to be on slippery ice.

* Chinese New Year Dragon Parade (also good for rhythm, timing and coordination)

> One to 3 children get under a small red cloth. The front child holds a dragon puppet. All children parade together around the room to Chinese music. Other children accompany music using triangles. Children take turns. This is a friendly dragon. Red means happiness.

* Reindeer Movement   (Partner Movement)

Discuss that reindeer are hitched together when pulling Santa's sleigh. They must all move at one time. "What would it be like to be attached to a partner and move together?" Hold hands with a partner. Give directions to walk or skip. Stress safety! Vary the activity for use with other themes.

    A.   Instead of holding hands, hold a scarf, colored ribbon or rope with partner.
    B.   Move together to music.
    C.   Hitch up like Santa's reindeer. Form line with pairs holding hands. Outside hand holds rope which reaches from first child to last child in line. Adult gives directions as above.
    D.   Some children can accompany with bells & rhythm sticks to be the "reindeer".

* Popcorn

Pretend to be a small, round kernel of popcorn. You are placed in a popcorn popper. The heat is turned on. You are getting hotter and hotter. Finally you pop and spread into a white popcorn which bounces up and down. Now you are all popped & still (relaxed), waiting to be eaten all up-yum!

* Listen and Do

Children should be spread out. Give simple instructions for children to follow:

Can you walk forward without touching anyone else?
Can you walk backward?
Show me how you walk sideways.
Can you slide sideways.
Gallop forward.
Hop forward.
Can you hop backward?
Hop sideways one way.
Hop sideways the other way.
Can you leap forward?
Jump forward.
Jump backward.
Jump to the side.
Use any other locomotion activities and stress that the children not touch anyone else.

Motor Planning

Through motor planning activities the children experience time, space, the logic of events and learn to make sense of their environment in relation to themselves (Casebeer, 1978). The children must first attend to the instructions, keep the total sequence in mind while attending to each detail in the correct order.

Motor Planning Activities

* Movement Sequences (This is excellent for sequential memory training.)

> Teacher verbally gives movement directions to a child or class and they attempt to respond in the correct order. For example, the teacher can say, "Take two steps forward, turn around, then clap twice", and so on.
>
> Place 2 tumbling mats end to end. Show children where the halfway line is. This can be done on the floor with a line marking the halfway point, or one mat can be used marking the halfway point.

> Creep halfway down the mats, turn and creep off backward.
> Roll sideways halfway down the mats, crawl off the other half.
> Take small standing bounces halfway down the mats forward, turn and bounce backwards down the other half.
> Knee-walk forward halfway down the mats, bunny jump backward to end.
> Crabwalk head first halfway down the mats, turn and crabwalk feet first the rest of the way. $\longrightarrow$

Seal crawl halfway down the mats, turn and
crabwalk feet first the rest of the way.
Frog-jump 2 jumps, roll sideways to end.
Crabwalk head first halfway down the mats,
then crawl forward the rest of the way.

* Cross the River   (also for locomotion & sequencing)

Child will cross the river (between two ropes) by
stepping or jumping on to colored "stones" made in
various shapes of paper or cardboard. The child
will be guided across the river by being told what
he should step on:

<u>First</u> step on the _____ .
<u>Next</u>, step on the _____ :
<u>Last</u>, step on the _____ .

(For <u>safety</u>, tape down paper or cardboard shapes)

* Things to Step Over

Use objects of varying heights: various shaped
boxes, ropes, blocks, balls, bean bags, small
wastepaper baskets, stacks of books and so forth.
Place the objects so that the children can step
over them without touching other objects.

Note: Four year olds should be able to step
over objects just enough to clear, but
younger children may step to an exaggerated
height to clear.

* Obstacle Courses

Obstacle courses can be made in the classroom or
on the playground. Every classroom should have
enough materials for an obstacle course--chairs,
boxes, tables, ropes, yardsticks, rug squares,
books. Arrange objects for going "under", "over",
"around", "on top of", "through", and "between",
for walking, hopping, crawling, tiptoeing, jumping, creeping.

. Walk the Challenge   (Lerch et al., 1974, p. 120)

Arrange hoops, tape, jump rope, balance beam, bean
bags, wands or other available equipment around
the room leaving plenty of space between.   →

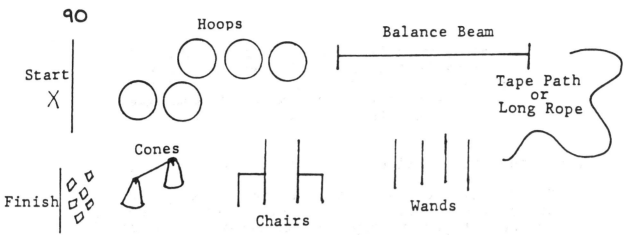

Hoops

Balance Beam

Start
X

Tape Path
or
Long Rope

Cones

Finish

Chairs

Wands

Bean Bags

Children move through, around, over or on the objects.

Directions may be called out as children move through the course, or given all at once at the beginning.

After skill improves, children may run through the course.

. Scooter Board (also good for balance)

Child will use scooter board in lying down or sitting position to push or pull with arms or feet around an obstacle course.

. Follow that Line!   (Casebeer, 1978, p. 95)

Paint or tape an obstacle course on the playground or in the room. Children will respond to the patterns.

. Following Big Foot

Have the children follow a pattern of "footprints" that have been cut out of sturdy paper; or, simply lay out squares of red and blue construction paper. If the latter method is used, tape a small piece of red construction paper or sticky dot on the right shoe and blue on the left shoe of each child walking the path. The children are to match the colors.

. Peter Cottontail's Bunny Trail

Pretend to be Peter Cottontail moving through obstacles on bunny trail to deliver Easter eggs. Examples of obstacles and ways to overcome them are:

Jump over or weave through blocks.
Circle around, weave through or crawl
  under chairs.
Jump or walk through tires.
Creep through boxes.
Go up stairs and come down slide.
Walk on balance beam.
Walk on two strings of yarn that are 6
  inches apart.
Walk on rope that is curved like a
  winding stream.

This activity can be done outside using a slide, cardboard boxes, tires, balance beam, etc. A course can be set up using tricycles or wagons (one or the other for safety).

Vary the activity for use with other themes: a farmer delivering food from the harvest for a 4th of July picnic or Thanksgiving, women or men astronauts delivering cargo to space stations, and so forth.

For primary children this activity can be used in conjunction with units on science, holidays, transportation & cultures (farming & transportation methods around the world), spelling (use letters in the obstacle course) or numbers (children add or subtract & write down their answers). The possibilities are limitless---check your curriculum and adapt this & other activities to enhance the children's learning. Have fun! Be creative! Let the children be involved in the creation-- thus developing leadership & self-esteem.

92

Children develop and use fundamental movement skills, not only while participating in planned movement activities, but also while engaging in free play on the playground. The design of a playground is an important factor in the development of these fundamental movement skills; in fostering self-esteem, independence, creativity and cognitive development; and in enhancing social and language skills.

Some of the important considerations in assessing and designing a playground are: safety factors, including weather conditions; developmentally appropriate equipment which includes all of the fundamental skill areas; multi-sensory materials which are easily accessible to the children; unstructured time for children to design their own activities; equipment for solitary play as well as for social groups of two to three children and larger group play; and traffic flow.

The playground design, as well as its use, need to foster cooperative, non-sexist play and be inclusive of special needs and multicultural children.

A well designed playground, which is combined with a supportive atmoshpere of the adults present and a creative, "free choice" use of a variety of materials will encourage children to have fun and develop to their full potential.

Note: There are many excellent articles and books which can be referred to for a more extensive study of this important topic. One such article is "How Can Playgrounds Be Improved? A Rating Scale," by Penny Lovell and Thelma Harms, Young Children (Journal), National Association for the Education of Young Children, 1834 Connecticut Ave., N.W., Washington, D.C. 20009, March, 1985. A copy of this article can be purchased from NAEYC for $2.

Illustrations include: catching, climbing, hanging, jumping, manipulation, running, throwing, balls, balance beam, tires, slide, stairs, swing & tree.

SKILL AREA V

MANIPULATION: THROWING, CATCHING, ROLLING,
KICKING, BOUNCING AND STRIKING

Manipulative activities, such as throwing, catching, kicking, bouncing and striking, require considerable coordination between the hands and eyes as well as the feet and eyes. Visual perception is very important in tracking the object and in determining its speed, distance and direction in relation to one's hands or feet. Through manipulative activities children can discover how objects travel: their direction, distance, rate of travel and size.

Many children are more willing to handle bean bags or lightweight balls such as Nerf balls, yarn balls, beach balls or balloons, because there is much less chance of getting hurt by them. As a result, the children will not develop an avoidance reaction to oncoming objects.

Throwing and Catching Activities

Overhand Throw Developmental Sequence.[*]

1. Feet remain stationary; body does not rotate; ball is thrown with forearm action.
2. Feet remain stationary; trunk rotates slightly; arm swings around the head in an oblique-horizontal plane.
3. A forward step with the leg on the same side of the body as the throwing arm is added to the pattern in #2.

---

[*]Adaptive Physical Education Department, Mount Diablo School District, 1981.

4. Mature pattern with trunk rotation, opposition in movement, and the elbow swings forward with the forearm extending and the wrist snaps, releasing the ball.

Underhand Throw Developmental Sequence.*

1. Feet stationary; ball tossed with forearm action only.
2. Feet stationary; underhand swing used.
3. Steps forward on the same side of the body as the arm swinging forward.
4. Knees flex as arm swings back; transfer of weight during throw and steps with opposition of movement.

Catching Developmental Sequence.*

Ground Ball:
1. Cannot catch at all.
2. Cannot position body in line with the ball.
3. Can position body in alignment but cannot "give" with the ball.
4. Can position body and catch ball successfully with hands.

Aerial Ball:
1. Cannot catch at all.
2. Turns head to avoid ball; waits for ball with arms straight and eyes closed.
3. Hands spread and arms straight while waiting for the ball; claps arms across chest when attempting to catch ball.
4. Clutches ball against chest and other body parts to keep hold of the ball.
5. "Gives" with the ball and catches with just the hands; knees slightly flexed.

* Pre-ball Skills

Throwing and catching are difficult skills for the young child. Catching scarves and balloons is much easier than catching fast balls.

. Scarves (also good for dance
          when done to music)
Demonstrate to a small group of children at a time how to throw a scarf up and catch it.   →

_____

*Adaptive Physical Education Department, Mount Diablo School District, 1981.

Let them practice. Throw the scarf under-hand. Tell the children to look at the cloth as you throw it to them, and to look at your hands as they throw it. Practice with both of them, then let them practice together. (A hand towel can be used in place of a scarf, but a towel will move faster.)

-Including music from many cultures benefits all the children while increasing self-esteem in the children from each culture. This also fosters an appreciation for many music styles.

. Scarf Game

Have no more than 4 children play. Demonstrate by throwing scarf up high and calling out a name in the group. The child whose name is called tries to catch the scarf before it hits the floor or ground. Children continue taking turns. (Colored ribbons or yarn can be used.)

. Balloon Volley   (Lerch et al., 1974, p. 112)

Inflate balloons with a penny or marble inside each balloon for weight. Be sure to have a few extras because some may burst. Children should be spread out and each child should have a balloon. The children should be encouraged to keep their eyes on the object being caught.

Can you throw your balloon into the air and catch it before it hits the ground?

Can you tap it lightly with both hands and keep it in the air? Keep tapping it to keep it up. Can you keep it up by tapping it with one hand? Be sure to keep your eyes on the balloon. Can you keep it up by tapping it with your other hand? Alternate hands, tap it first with one and then with your other. Keep your eyes on it.

Get a partner and tap the balloons back and forth to each other.   →

Can you tap your balloon
lightly against the wall
and keep it up?

Can you tap your balloon
high into the air and
catch it before it hits
the floor?

Toss the balloon into the air and see
how many times you can clap your hands
before you catch it.

Tap the balloon into the air. Can you
touch your knees and catch the balloon
before it hits the floor? Can you slap
your legs and then catch it? Can you
touch your toes and then catch it? Can
you clap your hands behind your back and
then catch it?

Can you keep the balloon in the air
hitting it with your head, elbows,
knees, feet?

. Jack-o-Lantern Catch

Carefully mark jack-o-lantern features on
orange balloon with permanent felt tipped
pen. Place a balloon into a kitchen funnel.
Toss balloon into air and attempt to catch it
with the funnel as it comes down.

* Bean Bag Activities

Bean bags are less frustrating and less threaten-
ing than balls because they will not roll away.
They are recommended for use in the classroom, but
can be used outside as well.

Have a variety of bean bags both in size and
weight. Three and 5 ounce bean bags work well.
Motor generalization is developed from a child
having to test the object weight and size.

Bean bags can be made into many different and
interesting shapes and colors (make all of one
kind the same weight):
birds, butterflies, spiders, bats, circles,
squares, triangles.
→

Each time a child uses a different bean bag it becomes a "new" activity, thus allowing for ample repetition without loss of interest.

. Bean Bag Throw and Catch Activities (Check skill level of child.)

Have the children:

- Throw the bean bag up in the air and catch it when it comes down.
- Throw it up and catch it with eyes closed.
- Holding two bean bags, throw them up simultaneously and catch them both.
- Throw the bean bag up and clap before it comes down.
- Throw one bean bag up, watch it and throw a second one up when one starts down. Keep juggling them.
- Throw a bean bag up and turn around before it comes down.
- Throw a bean bag back and forth to someone else. Move closer or farther apart for practice in changing force.
- Throw the bean bag underhand to a partner.
- Throw the bean bag overhand to a partner.
- Throw the bean bag back and forth from one hand to the other hand.
- Let bean bag fall from head and try to catch it.
- Throw bean bag up and catch it with both hands.

. Bean Bag Toss

Toss the bean bags into various objects. Use your imagination to tie these in with school themes. Each variation will be a "new" activity for the child and will allow for much repetition with high interest remaining.

Valentine Toss

Cut heart-shaped holes on one side of a large box. Stand appropriate distance away and throw two socks rolled together or bean bags into holes in various ways. Examples of ways to toss bags are: underhand, overhand, hike like a football. →

Variations:
Instead of box, use one of the following:

Toss heart-shaped bean bags into round holes on box.
Use bowls or pans of different sizes for targets with heart-shaped bean bags.
Tape heart-shaped targets on the floor.
Draw a heart-shaped target on butcher paper and place on floor.

Pumpkin Toss

Place plastic pumpkin container on floor. Stand designated distance from pumpkin and attempt to throw bean bag or small ball into container.

Ring the Christmas Bell

Hang a bell from the ceiling. Throw a bean bag or Nerf ball and try to "ring the Christmas bell."

Circle Toss

Child will toss bean bags into a rope circle on the floor, colored hoops, or large basket. Various pictures of snowmen, animals, airplanes or numerals, can be placed in the center for added interest. Vary the distance that the child stands from the circle.

Target Toss

A throwing target for bean bags can be made by stuffing an old pillowcase with rags or newspaper and suspending it from a line. Large paper bags, bicycle tires or tubes can also be suspended and used as targets.

Throw bean bag into wooden geometric shapes--designate which one.

* Ball Skills

Concentrate on ball activities requiring little
organization. Preschool children need the opportunity to just handle balls and learn basic ball
skills. Use a variety of balls, including light
balls, heavy balls, large balls, small balls and
different colored balls.

. Roll Ball

This is the most basic of all ball activities.
Two children sit on the floor with legs spread and
play a simple game by rolling the ball back and
forth to each other.

. Rolling Snow Balls

A 3 inch styrofoam "snow ball" is rolled to
children sitting in a circle. Call out the
child's name. He catches it and rolls it
after calling out another child's name.

. Bowling

Set up 1 quart sized plastic bleach bottles
for "pins" and have the children use a 6-inch
rubber ball to knock down the pins. Have
only 2 children play at a time; if more than
this play, it is too difficult for them to
wait for turns. The bleach bottles can be
weighted down with sand, pebbles, etc., but
be certain the tops are screwed on tight and
glued shut!

. Ping Pong Boat   (For safety this activity must be well
                       supervised.)
Float margarine tubs in water for boats.
Toss ping pong balls into boats. Repeat poem
while tossing ball:

    Ping pong boat.
    Ping pong boat.
    Ping pong in the boat.
    Watch it float.
Note: This activity can be done indoors using a water-
table or outside using a large tub or small pool.

. Peter Rabbit's Tail

> Draw outline of Peter Rabbit on large piece of paper. Draw circle marking location of rabbit's tail. Glue paper to side of Box. Stand rabbit upright. Make tail by rolling two white socks together, or use styrofoam ball. Toss socks at rabbit. The object is to throw tail as close to circle as possible.

. Target practice with Nerf ball and wastebaskets. Alternate with tennis balls or rings so children have the experience judging objects of different weights.

. Animal Toss

> Cut or draw large simple forms of animals or clowns from heavy cardboard or plywood. Holes of various sizes are cut out for the eyes, mouth, nose or in other places. The targets should be constructed with supports enabling them to stand alone, and can be painted in bright colors. Targets can also be taped to the wall without any holes cut out.

>> Stand in front of one of the targets. Can you throw your bean bag and make it go through one of the holes in the target? Can you throw it through the big holes? Can you throw it through the little holes?

> Ask child to aim for a partic-ular spot, such as the ele-phant's eye, the monkey's nose, the clown's right ear.

. Variety Toss

> Use a heavy cord with a variety of objects spaced and tied on it. This cord may then be tied between 2 posts or from one wall to another. For safety reasons, <u>make sure this is well above the children's heads</u>. Children stand about 6 feet away from the objects on

the cord and try to hit them with yarn balls, bean bags, or Nerf balls.

As skill improves, have children back farther away before they throw at the targets.

. Movement Exploration

Suggested questions:
-How low can you hold the ball?
-How high can you hold the ball?
-Can you take the ball even higher without letting go?
-If you want the ball to go even higher, what must you do?
-Can you do it another way?
-Who can bounce the ball with another part of the body? Another?
-Let's try using our feet. Who can sit down and hold the ball with their feet?
-Can you keep the ball there while you lift your feet?
-How many of you can hold the ball between your feet, lift your feet off the ground, and turn around in a circle?
-Show me how you can turn the other way.
-Can you hold the ball between your feet and put them over your head?
-Can you hold the ball in your hands or feet and make a human bridge?
-Now make a different shaped bridge.
-Can you place the ball on the floor and jump over it without touching it?
-Can you place the ball on the floor and jump over it? Can you jump higher?
-Who can jump backwards over the ball?
-Can you move the ball across the room using only your feet?

Kicking Activities

Kicking Developmental Sequence.*

Kicking in place
  1. Kicking leg nearly straight and involves very little body movement.

---

*Adaptive Physical Education Department, Mount Diablo School District, 1981.

2. Kicking leg lifted backward and upward in preparation for the kick; moves toward the ball.
3. Increased preliminary extension at the hip, greater arc in the leg swing and additional body adjustments; contacts the ball squarely.

Kicking while moving
1. Cannot align body with moving ball.
2. Aligns body but kicks over ball.
3. Aligns body but kicks ball with difficulty.
4. Aligns body with ball and kicks with a mature pattern.

Controlled kicking may not be accomplished until a child reaches the age of seven or eight. Preschool is the time to teach the child how to swing his legs, without expecting controlled kicking.

* Balloon Volley-Foot Style

    Have a blown-up balloon with a penny inside for each child. Use different color balloons.

    Lie down on your backs.
    Can you keep the balloon in
        the air using only your
        feet?
    How many times can you kick it
        before it lands on the
        floor?

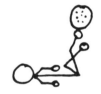

* Leg Swing

    Have children stand on one foot and put hands on hips, then swing legs backward and forward, first one leg and then the other. Next, have them try it with arms swinging freely. The legs should move in a smooth swing, back and forth, back and forth.

* Bean Bag Touch

    Have the children each hold a bean bag in one hand with arm extended forward. They kick each leg up, first one and then the other, and touch the hand holding the bean bag. Repeat using the other hand. Caution them not to kick the bean bag in the air. This can be another activity outdoors for those who are proficient.

* Bean Bag Lift

Have the children hold bean bags between their feet in a sitting position. They should raise their feet as high as they can without dropping the bag. Up, down, up, down.

* Ball Kick Exploration

Challenge child:

- -Can you kick with different parts of your foot? (toe, inside of foot, heel, outside of foot)
- -Can you kick in different directions? (forward, backward, sidewards)
- -Can you kick different types of balls? (soccer ball, football, wiffle ball, sponge ball)
- -Can you kick the ball _____? (as hard as you can, as soft as you can, with one foot, then the other, as far as you can, to a partner)

Bouncing Activities

Bouncing Developmental Sequence.*

1. Cannot bounce at all.
2. Bounces with little control; height varies.
3. Bounces ball in one place with some degree of control.
4. Bounces ball while moving, controlling direction and speed most of the time.
5. Good control of bouncing whether in place or while moving.

---

*Adaptive Physical Education Department, Mount Diablo School District, 1981.

* Bouncing Balls

   Eight-inch or 10-inch rubber balls are best for bouncing at the preschool age. Let each child experiment so he can learn how to make changes in position. Learning to bounce the ball from waist height with both hands is essential.

   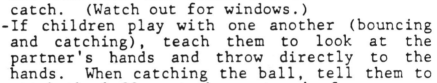

   -Child practices bouncing ball to self.
   -Let the child bounce balls against a wall--he can control his own ball and learn how to catch. (Watch out for windows.)
   -If children play with one another (bouncing and catching), teach them to look at the partner's hands and throw directly to the hands. When catching the ball, tell them to watch the ball, not the partner's face.
   -Teacher stands about 5 feet away and bounces ball once to child. Child bounces ball back 1 bounce. Teacher moves close (about 3 feet) and bounces once to child. Child bounces ball back 1 bounce. Repeat.
   -For older children, partners can bounce a tennis ball to each other (standing 8' apart). For safety, do this activity outside, avoiding window areas.

* Ring Bounce

   Child bounces ball into 3 rings. Various pictures can be placed inside to correspond with unit themes--rocketships, animals, valentines, colors, shapes and numerals.

* Number Bounce

   Place 5 rings on the floor with a numeral in the center of each (#1-5). Child will bounce ball the appropriate number of times near or in each ring.

Striking Activities

Striking Developmental Sequence.[*]

   1. Uses an extension of the forearm in swinging; steps forward in the same arm/same leg pattern.

---

[*]Adaptive Physical Education Department, Mount Diablo School District, 1981.

2. Strikes in a vertical plane; forward trunk bend; faces ball squarely.
3. Strikes in a horizontal plane; some trunk rotation and transfer of weight.
4. Mature pattern with trunk rotation, weight transfer and follow through.

Developmentally, most children do not learn to bat before the age of 8. Minimize batting activities. For example, limit batting to hitting balls on the ground with a plastic bat or hitting a suspended ball with the hand or with a racket.

* Balloon Hit

Hitting and chasing balloons is fun and gives the children practice in working with an extremely light object. Balloon hitting with partners is good practice.

See preball Activities under Throwing and Catching.

* Suspendable Ball (Lerch et al., 1974, p. 113)

Suspend a wiffle ball from the ceiling using a length of string. Ball should be about shoulder height. Allow space & a ball for each child.

Stand in front of ball. Can you reach out and touch it with your fingers?

Can you hit it gently with your hand?

Start the ball moving gently. Reach out and poke it using your finger. Try to poke it each time it swings back to you.

Push the ball to make it move. Can you stop it with your hand? Remember to keep your eyes on the ball.

Start the ball moving. Can you hit it with your hand? Hit it each time it swings back to you. Count the number of times you hit the ball. Watch the ball.

Pick up a paddle. Can you hit the ball with
the paddle? Remember to hit it gently and
keep your eyes on it.

For Kindergarten & Primary Children:

Start the ball moving. Pick up a paddle.
Can you hit the ball with the paddle? Hit it
each time it swings back to you. Count the
number of hits you get. Remember to keep your
eyes on the ball.

As children develop hand-eye coordination, a plastic bat
can be used to strike the swinging ball. When manipulative
skill improves, a smaller ball can replace the larger ball.
A plastic bat can be used to strike a ball which is placed
stationary on the ground or on a traffic-type cone.
For safety, use the playground for this activity and insure
that the "batter" has a large, clear space around him, with
other children standing away.

ORGANIZED GAMES
Low-level games provide an opportunity for children to
combine and practice the fundamental movement skills which
they have acquired. Cooperative games, where children
remain in the games rather than becoming "out", allow the
children to participate fully, meet with success and gain
self-esteem.

Manipulative, rhythm and circle games, chosen at the children's skill level, develop self-control, good sportsmanship
(cooperation) and social interaction.

Encouraging children to make up and organize their own
games provides opportunities for them to develop creativity
and leadership skills.

SKILL AREA VI

RHYTHM AND TIMING

Rhythm and timing are enjoyable movement experiences for most children and at the same time provide further opportunities to develop basic motor skills. Both rhythm and timing are essential elements in coordinated movement and, in turn, movement aids in the development of rhythmic abilities. Thus these interdependent areas can be combined effectively, enhancing both (Gallahue, 1976).

Rhythm involves a sense of timing, and the ability to relate motor activities to verbal commands, for example, putting movements to a song or chant. This is called auditory-motor match. A rhythm is established when a movement or verbal expression is repeated over and over again.

Rhythm and timing activities help develop listening skills, auditory memory abilities and the ability to inter-pret rhythm into movement (creativity). It fulfills an inherent need in children of all ages, serving as an excit-ing opportunity for creative self-expression through freedom of movement. Through rhythm, a child can experience the joy and exhilaration of moving in time to the beat of a drum or the tempo of a record.

Through fundamental rhythms each child learns to move effectively and efficiently by integrating different body parts into a smooth functioning whole. He develops a feeling of grace and poise which served to enhance feelings of self in relation to his capabilities (Lerch, et al., 1974).

Rhythm is an area of the curriculum in which all children can meet with success. It provides another opportunity for positive self-expression and growth in a most desirable manner.

Steady Beat

A steady beat is essential to rhythm and timing. Children should first use their own voices and bodies to establish steady beat by clapping, stomping, etc. They need to internalize steady beat before they are able to produce this on external things such as rhythm instruments. It is important for children to realize that <u>they</u> can make music. They themselves are musical instruments and do not need to rely on records or a piano, which should be used sparingly.

Steady Beat Activities

* Echo

Child or teacher selects a pattern such as follows and others repeat the rhythm pattern 4 times.

1 clap - 1 slap	3 claps - 1 slap
3 - 2	1 - 3
3 - 3	2 - 3
1 - 2	3 - 2
2 - 1	

* Name Clap

A simple activity such as "My name is __(clap)__" can establish a rhythm. "My name is Ann", repeated over and over, using accent and clapping hands, is easy, and the children love it. "My name is David." "My name is Christopher." Different rhythmic patterns will be established depending on the number of syllables in each child's name.

* Follow the Pattern

The teacher selects a specific movement pattern and rhythm. An example of such a movement pattern would be:
   1. slap knees
   2. pat stomach
   3. clap
   4. clap

* Finishing Rhymes

Teacher and children repeat a rhyme. The third time that the rhyme is repeated, the children come in with the last words as teacher stops. For example, "Hickory Dickory _____, the mouse ran up the _____." Start with familiar ones.

Or, as rhyme is said, certain words can be substituted by a clap or knee slap, "Hickory Dickory __(slap)__,..." Most preschool children love nursery rhymes.

* Move to the Beat (also for locomotion and common space)

Clap hands and walk around in circle to the beat.
Hop around circle in time to clapping beat.
Move around in a designated space in response to singing rhythm.
Clap time to singing rhythm while moving in circle or forward and back.
Move fast or slowly across room in response to tempo (varying) of piano, record or drum beat.

→

Walk around in circle to singing or drum and
   change direction on heavy or "special" beat (set
   by teacher).

* The Grand Old Duke of York (also good for direction
  and balance)

        The Grand Old Duke of York,
        He had ten thousand men.
        He marched them up to the top of the hill,
        And marched them down again.
        So when you're up, you're up,
        And when you're down, you're down,
        And when you're only half way up,
        You're neither up nor down.

Children stand and march with knees high during
first 4 lines, then go on tiptoes in response to
the word "up", squat to the word "down", and squat
half way to the words "half way".

* Bingo   (also good for sequencing & spelling--best for
          older preschoolers & primary children)
          There was a farmer had a dog, (cat, cow, duck..)
          And Bingo was his name-O.
          B-I-N-G-O, B-I-N-G-O, B-I-N-G-O,
          And Bingo was his name-O.

Begin by singing whole song and then repeating the
song, dropping the "o" in Bingo, substituting a
clap. Next time drop the "g" and substitute two
claps for the missing letters. Continue until
each letter of Bingo is dropped and the whole word
is clapped. For variety, change the dog's name:
S-P-O-T-O, G-I-N-G-E-R-O. It's fun to fit these into the
rhythm of the song.

* Miss Mary Mack (also for auditory-memory)

        Teacher: Miss Mary Mack
        Pupils: Mack, Mack
        Teacher: All dressed in Black
        Pupils: Black, black
        Teacher: With silver buttons
        Pupils: Buttons, buttons $\longrightarrow$

Teacher:	Up & down her back
Pupils:	Back, back
Teacher:	She asked her mother
Pupils:	Mother, Mother
Teacher:	For fifteen cents
Pupils:	Cents, cents
Teacher:	To see the elephants
Pupils:	Elephants, elephants
Teacher:	Jump the fence
Pupils:	Fence, fence
Teacher:	They jumped so high
Pupils:	High, high
Teacher:	They touched the sky
Pupils:	Sky, sky
Teacher:	And they never came down
Pupils:	Down, down
Teacher:	Till the Fourth of July
Pupils:	July, July

* Peanut-Peanut Butter-Jelly (also good for laterality,
crossing the midline, sequencing & auditory memory)
Kids love this!!!!

Chorus:
Peanut -- Peanut Butter -- Jelly
Peanut -- Peanut Butter -- Jelly

Verse 1:
First you get the peanuts
And you grind them, grind them.
Repeat verse.

Chorus.

Verse 2:
Next you get the grapes
And you crush them, crush them.
Repeat verse.

Chorus.

Verse 3:
Then you get the bread
And you spread it, spread it.
Repeat verse.

Chorus.

Verse 4:
Last you get the sandwich
And you eat it, eat it.
Repeat verse →

Chorus:
"Peanut Butter"
(Raise arms to-
gether to one
side diagonally
above shoulders
and say "Peanut--
peanut butter.")

Jelly:
(Lower arms
diagonally to one
side below waist
and say "Jelly" in
low voice.)

Verses:
Use appropriate
actions.

Chorus: Sing as though your mouth is stuck with
        peanut butter.
Say: I've got peanut butter stuck to the roof of
        my mouth.
        I've got to drink a glass of milk.
        Gulp - Gulp - Gulp - (pretend to drink)
        AH!

* This Is What I Can Do

    Tune: "Old MacDonald Had a Farm"
    Sing the following words while doing some movement
    (blink eyes, clap hands, shrug shoulders, jump up
    and down.)

        This is what I can do
        Everybody do it, too
        This is what I can do.
        Now I send it on to you...

When singing "on to you", name, point to, or tap a
child who then becomes the new leader, and song is
repeated. Until the children master the idea, the
teacher will have to help them to think of things
to "do."

* I'm a Little Teapot   (good for laterality and
  balance)

        I'm a little teapot   "Stand and put the beat
        Short and stout   in your knees and here
        Here is my handle   we go." (Keep bending
        Here is my spout   knees to accent the
        When I get all   beat.)
          steamed up
        Then I shout
        Just tip me over
        Pour me out.

    Repeat using other side
    as spout. Act out
    appropriate motions.

* Going on a Lion Hunt
  Keep up a steady beat alternating slapping knees--
  a walking tempo. Use appropriate motions.

        Chorus:
        I'm going on a lion hunt and I'm not afraid
        I'm going to catch a lion and I'm not afraid.
                                                    →

Do you want to go along?
Well come, let's go!
　　　Repeat chorus.

First we get our camera (put on shoulder).
And then we get our net (put over other
　shoulder).
　　　Repeat chorus.

Out the door (slam).
　　　Repeat chorus.

Oh dear, here is a stream.
Can't go over it, can't go under it.
We'll have to swim.
　　　Repeat chorus.

Oh Dear, tall grass.
Can't go over it, can't go under it.
We'll have to go through it.
　　　Repeat chorus.

Oh dear, a big swamp.
Can't go over it, can't go under it
Guess we'll have to wade.
　　　Repeat chorus.

Here's a tree. Let's climb it and see if we
　see a lion.
I don't see him, but there is a big black
　cave.
Let's see if he is there.
　　　Repeat chorus.

Here's the cave. Look inside. Feel around.
　Something warm. Something furry. It's a
　lion! Let's run! (Slap knees fast.)
Up the tree
Down the tree
Run
Through the swamp
Run
Through the tall grass
Run
Through the stream
Run
There's the house. Through the door. Slam.
　Whew!
We're not afraid!

114

Instruments

Children love using instruments and can become quite good with them. Before using instruments the children need extensive practice with steady beat on their own bodies, such as lap-clap patterning, while singing or chanting. Internal rhythm develops before external rhythm. Be sure to select songs which are familiar to the children so that they will have only one new element to deal with at a time.

The teacher should demonstrate each instrument and tell its name. Later the children can review this themselves.

The teacher should control the instruments by allowing one child at a time to select. She should collect the instruments in a controlled manner by going around the circle or by collecting all rhythm sticks first, then all triangles and so forth.

The teacher should allow time for each child to investigate his instrument and then have the child put it down in the rest position before beginning the song. This rest position can be also used at the end of the song.

Allow plenty of space between children so that each child can hear his own music and not be disturbed by another instrument.

Allow plenty of time so that all children have turns.

* Freeze (good for balance also)

    Children will walk to the beat of the drum or other instrument. Children "freeze" when beat stops.

* Moving Instruments (for balance and motor planning also)

    Select a variety of instruments to be used--bells, drums, rhythm sticks, or triangle. Tell the children that each instrument means that they move in a certain way. At first, limit the number of

movements. One of the instruments used should be
chosen as the "freeze" instrument, where upon
hearing this instrument, the children freeze at
once. Choose to have a specific number of counts
for each instrument--8 counts of ringing the bell,
followed by 4 beats on the drum. Older children
can compose their own works, selecting the instruments, timing, and the movement patterns.

* Play and Sing (good also for sequencing)

   Have children accompany their singing using
   various instruments. Be sure to select songs with
   a steady beat and which the children know well.
   -Each child chooses an insturment as the box of instruments is
   passed. Children can take turns passing & collecting them.

* Hide and Listen (good for auditory memory)

   After teacher demonstrates each instrument, she
   hides them behind a box or screen and plays one
   instrument as children guess which one was played.

* Name that Tune

   Teacher beats out the rhythm pattern of a familiar
   song or rhyme on drum or rhythm sticks. Children
   guess the name. Use one recently done.
   -Older children can take turns being the leader/"teacher".

Fingerplays--Repeat each finger play with the other body side "leading,"
            so that both sides of the body are developed equally!
Fingerplays and nursery rhymes are usually the first
verses that preschool children learn. Practice in
fingerplays strengthens finger muscles, develops
hand-eye control as well as rhyme and auditory memory.

* Santa Out

   Here is the chimney, (make fist enclosing thumb)
   Here is the top, (place palm of other hand on
     fist)
   Open the lid, (quickly remove top hand)
   And out Santa will pop. (pop up thumb)

* Santa Down

    Our chimney is small, (small circle)
    Old Santa's fat, (large circle)
    But he gets down (move hand downward)
    In spite of that.

* The Two Apples

    Way up in the apple tree (point upward with index
        finger)
    Two little apples smiled at me. (hold up 2
        fingers)
    I shook that tree as hard as I could (make shaking
        motions with hands and arms)
    And down came those apples! (hands sweep down and
        open wide)
    MMMMM! Were they good! (rub stomach)

* Fee, Fie, Foe, Fum

    See my finger, (point to index finger)
    See my thumb. (point to thumb)
    Fee, fie, foe, fum (point to each finger again)
    Finger's gone! (hide finger in fist)
    So is thumb! (hide thumb)

* The Train

    Choo, choo, choo, choo, (slide hands together)
    The train runs down the track. (run fingers down
        arm)
    Choo, choo, choo, choo, (slide hands together)
    And then it runs right back. (run fingers up arm)

* Six Little Ducks (Use appropriate actions.)

    Six little ducks that I once knew,
    Fat ones, skinny ones, fair ones too.,
    But the one little duck with the feather on his
        back,
    He led all the others with a quack, quack, quack.

$\longrightarrow$

He led all the others with a quack, quack, quack.
Down to the river they would go,
Wibble wobble wibble wobble to and fro.
But the one little duck with the feather on his
   back,
He led all the others with a quack, quack, quack.
He led all the others with a quack, quack, quack.

* I Had a Little Turtle (Use appropriate motions.)

    I had a little turtle who lived in a box.
    He swam in the river and climbed on the rocks.
    He snapped at the mosquitos.
    He snapped at the fleas.
    He snapped at the minnows.
    And he snapped at me.
    Well he caught the mosquitos.
    He caught the fleas.
    He caught the minnows.
    But he didn't catch me.

There are many, many others to be used! These are but
a few.

Rhythm and Timing/Body Parts

* Body Part Chants

    . Chant:
    (Do the movements with the words.)

        Let's count eyes...1, 2.
        Let's count ears...1, 2.
        Let's count your nose...1 nose.
        How about your chin...1 chin.
        Let's count feet...1, 2.
        Let's count hands...1, 2.
        Let's count your head...1 head.
        How about your stomach...1 stomach.

    This may be continued with all body parts being
    counted.

    . The children perform as the words are chanted in a
    group.

        2 little hands go clap, clap, clap.
        2 little feet go tap, tap, tap. $\longrightarrow$

```
2 little legs go jump, jump, jump.
1 little body turns around and around.
1 little child sits quietly down.
```

. Children perform as they hear the rhyme.

```
Reach to the ceiling; down to the floor.
Up to the ceiling and down once more.
Touch your nose.
Touch your toes.
Jump up and down,
Then turn around.
Sway in the breeze.
Bend your knees.
Shake, shake, shake,
Shake your head.
Close your eyes
Like you're in bed.
```

* My Eyes   (Suit actions to words.)

```
Here are my eyes,
One and two.
I give a wink,
So can you!
When they're open
I see the light;
When they're closed
It's dark like night.
```

* Busy Hands   (moderately slow)

```
Hands on shoulders, hands on knees.
Put them behind you, if you please.
Raise hands high up in the air,
Down at your sides; now touch your hair.
Hands on hips now you may place,
Touch your elbows; now your face.
Raise hands high up as before,
Now we'll clap--1, 2, 3, 4!
```

* All About Me

```
Here are my ears, here is my nose.
Here are my fingers, here are my toes,
Here are my eyes, both open wide.
```

→

Here is my mouth with teeth inside.
Here is my tongue that helps me speak,
Here is my chin, and here is my cheek.
Here are my hands that help me play,
Here are my feet for walking today.

* Movement Rhyme   (Casebeer, 1978, p. 63)

My hands upon my head I place,
Upon my shoulders, on my face.
At my waist and by my side,
Then behind me they will hide.
I will raise them way up high,
And like the birdies fly, fly, fly.
Then clap and clap, 1, 2, 3,
I will fold them quietly.
(Or, Please sit down so quietly,
Or, Turn around so quietly.)

* This Is the Way

Tune: "Here We Go 'Round the Mulberry Bush"
This is the way my arms go up,
My arms go up, my arms go up.
This is the way my arms go up,
So early in the morning.

This is the way my feet go out...
This is the way I nod my head...
This is the way I wiggle my nose...
This is the way I blink my eyes...

* Clap Your Hands

Clap your hands, clap your hands,
Clap them just like me!
Touch your shoulders, touch your shoulders,
Touch them just like me!
Tap your knees, tap your knees,
Tap them just like me!
Shake your head, shake your head,
Shake it just like me!
Clap your hands, clap your hands,
Now let them quiet be.

* Oliver Twist

> Oliver Twist, twist, twist,
> Can do this, this, this.
> Touch your toes, toes, toes!
> (Repeat)
> Touch your... (Add various body parts.
>   Children can take turns being Oliver
>   Twist.)

* This Old Man

> This old man, he played one (hold up one finger)
> He played knick-knack on my thumb (touch thumbs
>   rhythmically)
> With a knick-knack (tap knees twice)
> Paddy Wack (clap hands twice)
> Give a dog a bone, (extend one hand out)
> This old man came rolling home. (roll hands
> around each other)
>
> This old man, he played two (hold up two fingers
> He played knick-knack on my shoe (tap shoes)
> (Continue first verse)
>
> This old man, he played three (three fingers)
> He played knick-knack on my knee (tap knee)
>
> This old man, he played four (four fingers)
> He played knick-knack on my door (knock on
>   imaginary door)
>
> This old man, he played five (five fingers)
> He played knick-knack on my hive (make shape with
>   hands)

* I'm Being Swallowed by a Boa Constrictor

> I'm being swallowed by a boa constrictor,
> I'm being swallowed by a boa constrictor,
> I'm being swallowed by a boa constrictor and
>   I don't like it very much.
> Oh no, oh no, he swallowed
>   my toe,
>   He swallowed my toe.
> Oh gee, oh gee, he's up to
>   my knee.
>   He's up to my knee.

→

Oh me, oh me, he's up to my thigh.
    He's up to my thigh.
Oh giddle, oh fiddle, he's reached my middle,
    He's reached my middle.
Oh heck, oh heck, he's swallowed my neck,
    He's swallowed my neck.
Oh dread, oh dread, he's swallowed my
Gulp

* My Hands

On my head my hands I place,
On my shoulders, on my face.
On my hips, at my side.
Then behind me they will hide.
Put my hands up so high,
Make my fingers quickly fly.
Put my hands in front of me,
Swiftly clap, 1, 2, 3!

* Flying Finger, Flying Feet
(Children need to have plenty of space.)

Flying fingers, flying high
Flying way up to the sky.
Flying fingers, flying low
Find a place you like to go.
(Everyone lies on their backs.)
Flying feet, flying high
Flying way up to the sky.
Flying feet, flying low
Find a place you like to go.

* Open, Shut Them

Open, shut them, open shut them
Give a little clap.
Open, shut them, open shut them
Put them in your lap.
Creep them, creep them, creep them, creep
  them
Way up to your chin.
Open up your little mouth, but do not
  let them in!
(The fingers quickly fly behind the back.)

* Winter Freeze

      Zip up your coat, (pretend to zip)
      And put on your hat. (pat top of head)
      Mr. South Wind is taking a nap. (rest head
         on hands) (Mrs. South Wind)
      Mr. North Wind will nip at your nose, (point
         to nose) (Mrs. South Wind)
      And Freeze your fingers (wiggle fingers)
      And your toes. (wiggle toes)

   Note: Can be used with study of science and cultures.

* Santa Claus

      Santa Claus is big and fat.
        (form large circle with
        arms)
      He wears black boots (point to
        feet)
      And a bright red hat   (point
        to head)
      His nose is red (point to
        nose)
      Just like a rose,
      And he ho, ho, hoes,
      From his head to his toes.
        (point to head and toes)

* Put Your Finger in the Air   by Woody Guthrie

      Put your finger in the air, in the air,
      Put your finger in the air, in the air,
      Put your finger in the air,
      Tell me, how's the air up there?
      Put your finger in the air, in the air.

      Put your finger on your head...
      Tell me, is it green or red?...

      Put your finger on your cheek...
      And leave it about a week...

      Put your finger on your ear...
      And leave it about a year...

      Put your fingers all together...
      And we'll hope for better weather...

* What Can You Do, Mr. Rabbit?
  Tune: "Frere Jacques

          What can you do, Mr. Rabbit?
          Here at school,
          Here at school?
          I can __wiggle my nose__.
          I can __wiggle my nose__.
          Here at school,
          Here at school.

One player stands in front of group and does action which is sung in verse. Examples of actions: wiggle my ears, hop on two feet, chew my carrot.

Repeat with different leader choosing new action.

Rhythm and Timing/Coordination

* Follow Me in a Line (good for balance also)

          Follow me in a line,
          In a line, in a line.
          Follow me in a line,
          And we'll go this way.

Form line. Sing verse while following leader who can walk, hop, or skip around room. At the end of the verse, the leader freezes in an unusual or peculiar position. Followers then freeze in the same position. Change leaders and repeat.

* What I Found under the Christmas Tree

    I found a ball under the
      Christmas tree.
    And this is the way it
      bounced for me.
    Bounce, bounce, bounce.
    And this is the way it
      bounced for me.

  Variations
    In place of ball bounced,
    use the following:
    -Doll, and this is the way she talked to me.

                                    ⟶

Ma-ma-ma-ma.
-Top, and this is the way it spun for me. Spin,
spin, spin.
-Rocking horse, and this is the way it rocked for
me. Rock, rock, rock.
-Piano, and this is the way it played for me.
Tra-la-la-la.
-Horn, and this is the way it tooted for me.
Toot-toot-toot-toot.

* If You're Happy and You Know It

If you're happy and you know it, clap your hands.
If you're happy and you know it, clap your hands.
If you're happy and you know it
Then your face will surely show it.
If you're happy and you know it, clap your hands.

If you're mad and you know it, stomp your feet.
If you're mad and you know it, stomp your feet.
If you're mad and you know it
Then your face will surely show it.
If you're mad and you know it, stomp your feet.

If you're sad and you know it, cry some tears.
If you're sad and you know it, cry some tears.
If you're sad and you know it
Then your face will surely show it.
If you're sad and you know it, cry some tears.

If you're excited and you know it, shout "hooray."
If you're excited and you know it, shout "hooray."
If you're excited and you know it
Then your face will surely show it.
If you're excited and you know it, shout "hooray."

* Windshield Wipers

Windshield wipers are important when driving in a
car while it is raining. We could not see without
them. Let's pretend to be wipers by extending our
arms upward and bending side to side.

When I drive with Dad and Mom
And the rain comes splashing down ;
Dad (Mom) turns on a button then
The wipers come zooming on.
SPLISH, SPLASH, SPLISH, SPLASH.

→

Back and forth and back and forth,
They swish across the glass.
It's fun to watch, but won't last long.
For the storm will quickly pass.

Rhythm and Timing/Relaxation

* Raggedy Doll (also for coordination and body parts)
  (Franz, Note 3)

    The Raggedy doll said, "I don't mind
    If my pants are held with a pin behind,
    Or that the sawdust is out of my toe--
    'Cause I'm just a raggedy doll, you know."

    "My arms are so floppy, they fling and flap,
    And my head rests all the way down in my lap."

    "The rest of me goes to and fro--
    'Cause I'm just a raggedy doll, you know."

    "If somebody pulled me up by a string,
    I'd stand so straight I'd certainly sing.
    But my legs are so wobbly they just let go--
    "Cause I'm just a raggedy doll, you know."

    "I can't move a muscle--I can just smile,
    I just have to stay here for a long, long while."

    "I feel so soft from my head to my toe--
    "Cause I'm just a raggedy doll, you know."

* Baby Birdies (Also for coordination)
  (Act out following verse)

    We are baby birdies
       living in a nest.
    We dream of flying when
       we take our rest.
    Finally one spring day we
       hop, hop, hop.
    And flutter our wings
       flop, flop, flop.
    They lift us up and then
       we fly.
    We fly all around the
       sky.
    Flying very high and
       flying very low.
    Then in a big circle--round we go. ⟶

Finally we soar home and to sleep.
We close our eyes without a peep.

* Fall Tree (also for coordination)

Today we are going to pretend we are big, tall
trees. Stretch our limbs to make the branches.
It is fall of the year, and we start to lose our
leaves.

    Little leaves fall gently down (pretend to be
       leaves)
    Red and yellow, orange and brown.
    Whirling, whirling round and round,
    Quietly without a sound, (whisper)
    Falling softly to the ground.
    Down and down and down and down.
    Along comes a child to rake the leaves.
       (pretend to be child)
    I rake and rake the leaves,
    Into a great big hump.
    And then I stand back of it,
    Bend both knees and jump.

Rhythm and Timing/Balance

* Ring Around the Rosy (also good for balance)

    Children clasp hands and form a circle; they walk
    to the right or left.

    Ring around the rosy, pocket full of posy
    Ashes, ashes, we all fall down! (in a squat)
    or
    One, two, three and squat where you be!

* Tiptoe Activities

  . Butterflies (Tune: "Hush Little Baby/Mama's Gonna
    Buy You a Mockingbird")

        I spread my wings like a butterfly,
        Up and down and low and high.
        I spread my wings and I fly all day,   →

Up and down and far
    away!

.   More   Butterflies   (Tune:
"Row, Row, Row Your Boat")

        Fly, fly, butterfly
        Way up in the sky,
        Fly, fly, fly with me
        Way up to the tree!

.   I'm Bouncing (Tune: "Skip to My Lou")

        I'm bouncing, bouncing everywhere,
        I bounce and bounce into the air,
        I'm bouncing, bouncing like a ball,
        I bounce and bounce, and then I FALL!

Rhythm and Timing/Locomotion

    * See Crawling Activities.

    * See Creeping Activities.

    * Jack Be Nimble

            Jack be nimble, Jack be quick,
            Jack jump over the candlestick.

        Circle game. Place a cardboard roll or wooden
        block for the candlestick in center of circle.
        One child is chosen to be Jack who jumps over the
        candlestick while verse is recited. Choose new
        Jack and repeat.

        Variation
            Form line and take turns jumping over a
            wooden block. After all have had a turn,
            increase height by adding additional blocks.
            Repeat.

    * Frog Jump (also good for balance)

        Children squat and place hands flat on floor or
        grass between their legs. They should push with
        their toes and hop forward with their hands moving

slightly ahead of their feet, then land on their feet in a squating position again.

Chant: A little frog in a pond am I,
          Hippity, hippity hop!
          I can hop in the air so high,
          Hippity, hippity, hop!

* Can You Be a Rabbit?

Act out following verse:

Can you be a rabbit with two ears so very long?
Can you hop, hop, hop about on legs so small and strong?
You nibble, nibble carrots for your dinner every day.
As soon as you have had enough you scamper far away.

* Hop, Hop, Hop

Hop in different ways while saying verse.

Find a foot and hop, hop, hop.
When we're tired we stop, stop, stop.
Turn around and count to ten.
Find a foot and hop again.

* Whoops!   (good also for balance, space and direction)
  (Tune: "Here We Go 'Round the Mulberry Bush")

Have the children circle around to the right, hands joined. Everyone sing:

We circle and circle around the chairs,
Around the chairs around the chairs,
We circle and circle around the chairs
On a ___(Monday)___ morning--WHOOPS!

When they say "Whoops!" they all jump up, then squat down together.

Repeat with: around the room, the toys, Suzi, etc.

* Witch

> If I were a witch I'd ride on a
>   broom (pretend to ride broom)
> And scatter ghosts with a zoom, zoom, zoom!
>   (pushing motion with arm)

* London Bridge (good for balance and motor planning)

> Pairs of children make a bridge by joining hands
> above head. Children can use various methods of
> locomotion to go under the bridge: creep, walk or
> animal walks.

* Elephant Walk (good also for balance)

> Children keep their knees straight, bend at hips,
> clasp hands together, and swing arms back and
> forth for the trunk. Steps are giant steps, slow
> and heavy.

> Chant: Right foot, left foot, see me go.
>   I am gray and big and slow.
>   I come walking down the street
>   With my trunk and four big feet.

* Turkey Walk (Tune: Did You Ever See a Lassie")

> Children hold their heads up high, puff out
> chests, tuck hands under their arms. They strut
> forward with knees straight and flap elbows for
> wings.

> Oh, gobble, gobble, gobble,
> Fat turkeys, fat turkeys,
> Oh, gobble, gobble, gobble,
> Fat turkeys are we.
> We strut very proudly we gobble so loudly,
> Oh, gobble, gobble, gobble,
> Fat turkeys are we.

Rhythm and Timing/Spatial Relationships

* Open, Close Them (also for developing strength)

> Open, close them,   (hold hands in front,
> Open, close them,   spread fingers apart,
> →

Give your hands a clap!   then close to make a
Open, close them,   fist)
Open, close them,
Now lay them in your lap.

* Ten Little Fingers #1 (also for developing strength)

    I have ten little fingers,
    And they all belong to me,
    I can make them do things,
    Would you like to see?

    I can hold them up high.
    I can hold them down low.
    I can put them behind me where they don't even
        show.
    I can wiggle them fast.
    I can wiggle them slow.
    I can put them in my lap, just so.

* Ten Little Fingers #2 (also for developing strength)

    I have ten little fingers (hold hands in front,
        spread fingers)
    And they all belong to me (point to self)
    Would you like to see?
    I can shut them up tight (bring fingers together)
    Or open them wide (spread fingers apart)
    I can put them together (bring together again)
    Or make them all hide. (make fist with thumb
        tucked in)
    I can make them jump high, (fling hands up)
    I can make them go low. (bring hands down)
    I can fold them quietly. (fold hands in lap)

* The Itsy Bitsy Spider (Use appropriate motions.)

    The itsy bitsy spider climbed up the water spout
    Down came the rain and washed the spider out.
    Out came the sun and dried up all the rain.
    And the itsy bitsy spider climbed up the spout
        again.

* Sledding

    Here's a hill (make hill
        with left arm)
    All covered with snow. →

We'll get on our sled
And ZOOM! Down we'll go!
   (swoop right hand downward)

* My Turtle

   This is my turtle (make fist, thumb extended)
   He lives in a shell (hide thumb in fist)
   He likes his home very well
   He pokes his head out (thumb out)
   When he wants to eat,
   And pulls it back in (thumb in)
   When he wants to sleep.

* Big Fat Turkey

   Our turkey is a big fat bird, (make circle with
     hands)
   His red chin always drooping down. (point to
     chin)
   He waddles when he walks, (place hands on
     shoulders and move elbows up and down)
   His tail is like a spreading fan, (link thumbs and
     spread fingers)
   And on Thanksgiving Day
   He sticks his tail up in the air
   And whoosh, he flies away. (pretend to fly away)

* Little Peter Rabbit
  (Tune: "The Battle Hymn of the Republic")

     Little Peter Rabbit had a <u>fly</u> upon his <u>nose</u>,
     <u>Little Peter Rabbit</u> had a <u>fly</u> upon his <u>nose</u>,
     <u>Little Peter Rabbit</u> had a <u>fly</u> upon his <u>nose</u>,
     And so he <u>flipped</u> and <u>flopped</u> it and it <u>flew</u>
      away.

   Each time the word "rabbit" is said, the child
places his hands at the top of his head to represent
ears; for the words "fly" and "flew" he makes flying
motions with his hand; each time the word "nose" is
said, he touches his nose; on the words "flipped" and
"flopped" he makes a flipping motion with his hands.
After the song and the motions are well known, have
child leave out the underlined words and fill in with
the motions.

* A-Tisket, A-Tasket

      A-tisket, a-tasket,
      A red and yellow basket
      Sent a valentine to my friend
      And on the way I dropped it.
      One of you has picked it up
      And put it in your pocket.

Circle game. While verse is sung, player A walks
around circle with a bean bag or heart. He drops
heart behind player B when fourth line is sung.
Player B picks up the heart and chases player A
around the circle to the empty space. Repeat.

* Friend of Mine (Tune: "Mary Had a Little Lamb")

      Will you be a friend of mine, a friend of mine, a
        friend of mine?
      Will you be a friend of mine and ___(action)___
        around with me?
      ___(Child's name)___ is a friend of mine, a friend
        of mine, a friend of mine.
      ___(Child's name)___ is a friend of mine who
        ___(action)___ around with me.

Circle game. One player moves around circle doing
action. Examples of actions are: skipping, hopping,
running. Player stops by another child and both
players move around circle. First player then sits
in circle and game is repeated with second child
moving around circle doing different action.

* Picking up Easter Eggs
  Tune: "Way Down Yonder in the Pawpaw Patch")

      Where, oh where, are the Easter
        eggs?
      Where, oh where, are the Easter
        eggs?
      Where, oh where, are the Easter
        eggs?
      Hidden out here in our back yard.
      Picking up ___(color)___ eggs, put them in the
        basket.
      Picking up ___(color)___ eggs, put them in the
        basket.
                                              →

Picking up   (color)   eggs, put them in the
    basket.
Hidden out here in our back yard.

While singing first part of verse, players place
hands above eyes and search for eggs. Players then
pretend to pick up eggs and place them in a basket.
Change color of eggs and repeat verse. Colored
plastic eggs are fun to use.

* Easter Bunny Comes to My House
  (Tune: "Bluebird, Bluebird Through My Window")

> Easter bunny comes to my house.
> Easter bunny comes to my house.
> Easter bunny comes to my house.
> To bring an Easter egg.

Circle game. Bunny walks around outside of circle
and stops in front of nearest player at end of
verse. Bunny asks child, "What color Easter egg
would you like?" Child answers, I would like
a   (color)   egg." Everyone sings, " (Child's
name)   would like a   (color)   egg." Child then
becomes Bunny and game is repeated. Variation:
Bunny holds basket with different colored eggs in
it. He gives child the color of egg he likes.
When child becomes Bunny he receives basket and
places his egg in it.

* Planting Pantomine #1
  (Act out following verse.)

> I plant a little seed in the dark, dark
>   ground. (pretend to be seed by crouching
>   on the floor and covering head with arms)
> Out comes the yellow sun, big and round.
>   (remain crouching, extend arms over head
>   and form large circle)
> Down comes the cool rain, soft and slow.
>   (flutter fingers)
> Up comes the little plant (pretend to be
>   growing plant)
> Grow, grow, grow. (stretch arms above body)

Ask each child to describe the kind of plant he
has become.

* Planting Pantomine #2

      I dig a hole and plant a seed. (pretend to
        plant seed)
      Cover it with dirt and pull a weed. (pretend
        to cover hole and pull weed)
      Down comes the rain and out comes the sun.
        (flutter fingers, form circle)
      Up grows my plant. Oh! What fun! (pretend
        to grow)

* My Hands (good also for body parts)

      I raise my hands up high
      Now on the floor they lie
      Now high, now low
      Now reach up to the sky.

      I spread my hands out wide
      Now behind my back they hide
      Now wide, now hide
      Now I put them at my side.

      I give my head a shake, shake, shake,
      Now, not a move I make
      Now shake, shake, shake
      Not a move I make
      Now my whole self I shake.

Jumping Rope: For Kindergarten & Primary Children.
    (good also for dynamic balance, jumping, manipulation,
    sequencing & steady beat)
    Have beginners jump without chanting. As skill with the
    jump rope improves, children can use traditional chants
    or activities found under rhythm & timing-steady beat
    to accompany their jumping.

    Traditional Chant For Jumping Rope (use nonsexist approach)
    Mother, Mother, am I ill?   (Father, father...)
    Call the doctor over the hill.
    In came the doctor, in came the nurse, (both female & male)
    In came the lady with the alligator purse.
    "Measles", said the doctor. "Mumps", said the nurse.
    "Nothing", said the lady with the alligator purse

Acting Out Fingerplays & Songs (good also for body awareness,
        balance, locomotion, manipulation & steady beat)
    Whenever possible have the children stand up & act out familiar finger-
    plays & songs. This reinforces fundamental skills as well as develop-
    ing creativity & leadership skills.
    Sitting in Circle Time: Use large arm motions with fingerplays & songs so that
      the arms cross the midline. (good for upper body strength)

Adaptive Physical Education Department. Motor skill devel-
    opment: Adaptive physical education inservice
    training for special day class. Concord, California:
    Mount Diablo School District, 1981.

Ball, T. S. Itard, Itard, Sequin and Kephart--sensory
    education--A learning interpretation. Columbus, Ohio:
    Merrill Publishing Co., 1971.

Bennett, C., Planning for activity during the important
    preschool years. Journal of Physical Education and
    Recreation. 1980, 51(7), 30-32.

Brigance, A. Brigance diagnostic inventory of early
    development. North Bellerica, Massachusetts: Curriculum
    Associates, Inc., 1978.

Capon, J. Perceptual-motor lesson plans. Alameda,
    California: Front Row Experience, 1975.

Casebeer, B. Casebeer program: Developing motor skills for
    early childhood education. Novato, California: Academic
    Therapy Publications, 1978.

Cassell, D. Traveling program works to develop motor
    skills. Day Care and Early Education 1979, 7(1), 52-53.

Cherry, C. Think of something quiet. Belmont, California:
    Pitman Learning, Inc., 1981.

Cratty, B. J., Ikeda, N., Martin, M., Jennett, C., & Morris,
    M. Movement activities, motor ability and the education
    of children. Springfield, Illinois: Thomas, 1970.

Erikson, E. Childhood and society. New York: Norton &
    Co., Inc., 1963.

Felton, V., and Peterson, R. Piaget: A handbook for
    parents and teachers of children in the age of discovery:
    Preschool-third grade. Moraga, California: Mulberry
    Tree Preschool, 1976.

Furth, H., & Wachs, H. Thinking goes to school: Piaget's
    theory in practice. New York: Oxford University Press,
    1975.

Gallahue, D. Developmental movement experiences for child-
    ren. New York: John Wiley and Sons, Inc., 1982.

Gallahue, D. Motor development and movement experiences for
    young children (3-7). New York: John Wiley and Sons,
    Inc., 1976.

Godfrey, B., & Kephart, N. Movement patterns and motor education. New York: Appleton, Century and Crofts, 1969.

Kephart, N. The slow learner in the classroom. Columbus, Ohio: Charles Merrill Books, Inc., 1960.

Lerch, H., Becker, J., Ward, B., & Nelson, J. Perceptual-motor learning: Theory and practice. Palo Alto, California: Peek Publications, 1974.

Lipson, A. Catching them early. Academic Therapy. March 1981, 16(4), 457-462.

Lovell, P., & Harms, T. How can playgrounds be improved? A rating scale. Young Children. March, 1985, 3-8.

Piaget, J. The origins of intelligence in children. New York: International Universities Press, Inc., 1952.

Skinner, L. Motor development in the preschool years. Springfield, Illinois: Charles C. Thomas, 1979.

Spache, E. Reading activities for child involvement. Boston: Allyn & Bacon, Inc., 1982.

Van Oteghen, S., & Jacobson, P. Preschool individualized movement experiences. Journal of Physical Education, Recreation and Dance. May, 1981, 52(5), 24-26.

REFERENCE NOTES

1. Capon, J. Rationale for perceptual-motor programs. Paper presented at movement education workshop, Walnut Creek, California, January 1981.

2. Casebeer, B. Telephone interview. January 1981.

3. Franz, K. Movement workshop. Paper presented at workshop, Oakland, California, April 1982.

RECORDS

Bowmar Records, Inc., 622 Rodier Drive, Glendale, California 91201
    Rhythm Time, Album B301, Lucille Wood
    Rhythm Time #2, Album B 302, Lucille Wood

Warner Brothers, Los Angeles, California
    Peter, Paul and Mommy, Album 1785, Peter Paul and Mary

APPENDIX A

SEQUENCE OF EMERGENCE OF SELECTED
MOVEMENT ABILITIES

Adapted from MOTOR DEVELOPMENT AND MOVEMENT EXPERIENCES FOR YOUNG CHILDREN (3-7)
by David Gallahue, 1967. Reprinted by permission of John Wiley & Sons, Inc.

MOVEMENT PATTERN	SELECTED ABILITIES	APPROXIMATE AGE OF ONSET
DYNAMIC BALANCE	Walks 1-inch straight line . . .	3 years
	Walks 1-inch circular line . . .	4 years
	Stands on low balance beam . . .	2 years
	Walks on 4-inch wide beam short distance	3 years
	Walks on same beam, alternating feet	3-4 years
	Walks on 2- or 3-inch beam . . .	4 years
	Performs basic forward roll. . .	2 years
	Performs mature forward roll . .	6-7 years
STATIC BALANCE	Pulls to a standing position . .	10 months
	Stands without handholds	11 months
	Stands alone	12 months
	Balances on one foot 3-5 seconds.	5 years
	Supports body in basic inverted positions.	6 years
WALKING	Rudimentary upright unaided gait	13 months
	Walks sideways	16 months
	Walks backward	17 months
	Walks upstairs with help	20 months
	Walks upstairs alone--follow step	24 months
	Walks downstairs alone--follow step	25 months
RUNNING	Hurried walk (maintains contact)	18 months
	First true run (nonsupport phase)	2-3 years
	Efficient and refined run. . . .	4-5 years
	Speed of run increases	5 years

138

JUMPING	Steps down from low object . . .	18 months
	Jumps down from object with both feet.	2 years
	Jumps off floor with both feet .	28 months
	Jumps for distance (about 3 feet).	5 years
	Jumps for height (about 1 foot).	5 years

HOPPING	Hops up to 3 times on preferred foot	3 years
	Hops from 4 to 6 times on same foot	4 years
	Hops from 8 to 10 times on same foot	5 years
	Hops distance of 50 feet in about 11 seconds	5 years
	Hops skillfully with rhythmical alteration	6 years

| GALLOPING | Basic but inefficient gallop . . | 4 years |
| | Gallops skillfully . . . . | 6 years |

SKIPPING	One-footed skip.	4 years
	Skillful skipping (about 20 percent).	5 years
	Skillful skipping for most . . .	6 years

THROWING	Body faces target, feet remain stationary, ball thrown with forearm.	2-3 years
	Same as above but with body rotation added	3.6-5 years
	Steps forward with leg on same side as throwing arm	5-6 years
	Mature throwing pattern.	6.6 years

CATCHING	Chases ball; does not respond to aerial ball	2 years
	Responds to aerial ball with delayed arm movements.	2-3 years
	Needs to be told how to position arms.	2-3 years
	Fear reaction (turns head away).	3-4 years
	Basket catch using the body. . .	3 years
	Catches using the hands only with a small ball.	5 years

KICKING	Moves against ball. Does not actually kick it	18 months
	Kicks with leg straight and little body movement (kicks <u>at</u> the ball)	2-3 years
	Flexes lower leg on backward lift	3-4 years
	Greater backward and forward swing with definite arm opposition	4-5 years
	Mature pattern (kicks <u>through</u> the ball).	5-6 years
STRIKING	Faces object and swings in a vertical plane	2-3 years
	Swings in a horizontal plane and stands to the side of the object	4-5 years
	Rotates trunk and hips and shifts body weight forward . .	5 years
	Mature horizontal patterns . . .	6-7 years

APPENDIX B

GLOSSARY
TERMS ASSOCIATED WITH MOVEMENT EDUCATION

Adapted from Capon (1975), Skinner (1979),
and Franz (Note 3)

AUDITORY-MOTOR: The ability to relate verbal commands to motor activities, and to a sense of timing.

BALANCE: The ability to assume and maintain any body position against the force of gravity; resulting from the interaction of the muscles working to keep the body on it's base.

> DYNAMIC BALANCE: The ability to maintain equilibrium while the body is in motion.

> OBJECT BALANCE: The ability to balance other materials on one's body.

BODY AWARENESS: Involves the knowledge of: (a) the physical structure of body parts; (b) the movements and functions of body parts; and (c) the ability to coordinate body parts so as to move in an efficient manner.

COORDINATION: Control of one's body, muscle control, balance and awareness of the different parts of the body.

> FINE MOTOR COORDINATION: Small muscle control.

> GROSS MOTOR COORDINATION: Large muscle control.

DIRECTIONALITY: Often confused with laterality. An awareness of space outside of the body and involves: (a) knowledge of directions in relation to right and left, in and out, and up and down; (b) the projection of one's self in space; and (c) the judging of distance between objects.

FOOT-EYE COORDINATION: Refers to one's ability to use feet and eyes together to accomplish a task.

HAND-EYE COORDINATION: Refers to one's ability to use hands and eyes together to accomplish a task.

ISOMETRICS (ISOMETRIC EXERCISES): Exercise involving contraction of the muscles without observably moving them.

KINESTHESIS: Refers to the sensations (or messages) the central nervous system receives through the muscles, joints, tendons and related structures that inform one of body movements and positions. Kinesthetic: adjective form of kinesthesis.

LATERALITY: Sideness; an internal awareness of the two sides of the body.

    BILATERAL: Refers to the use of both sides ·(or halves) of the body.

    CROSS-LATERAL: Refers to the working together of different limbs on opposite sides of the body.

    UNILATERAL: One-sided; using one side only.

LOCOMOTION: The ability to move oneself from one place to another.

MID-LINE: Center of the body vertically; dividing line between right and left sides of the body.

MOTOR LEARNING: Apparently permanent change in motor performance brought about through practice and excluding change from maturation.

MOTOR PLANNING: The ability of the brain to conceive of, organize, and carry out a sequence of unfamiliar actions.

MOTOR SKILL: A movement or limited series of movements performed with a high degree of precision for the accomplishment of a specific end.

MOVEMENT EDUCATION: The study or learning process which deals with development and training in basic movement skills.

MOVEMENT EXPLORATION: A method and process of teaching and learning movement in which the individual is guided or proceeds through progressively less teacher-directed and more self-directed experiences designed to elicit his own movement patterns in relation to his personal capabilities.

MOVEMENT PATTERN: The external or outwardly observable basic movements an individual performs in handling the body alone and/or in handling objects.

PERCEPTION: Interpretation and analyzation by the brain of the information coming through the senses (visual, auditory, tactile, kinesthetic).

PERCEPTUAL-MOTOR: The processing of information coming into the central nervous system through the senses and making appropriate motor responses.

POSTURE: Position in space--static or dynamic in which a series of muscle groups move so that the position of the body, with reference to its center of gravity, is maintained.

PSYCHOMOTOR: Muscular activity associated with the total emotional and intellectual responses of an individual to his environment.

READINESS: Willingness, desire and ability to engage in a given activity, depending on the learner's level of maturity, previous experience, and mental and emotional set. Prepared or set for something.

RHYTHM: Control of time and energy. Temporal-force component of movement.

SENSORY-MOTOR (SENSORIMOTOR): The combination of the input of sensations to the central nervous system, the processing of the information and the output of appropriate muscular activity.

SEQUENCE: Ordering of events on the temporal scale; relation of movement acts one to the other in time.

SPACE: The area on the ground (or in the air or water) occupied by the body or its parts at any one time. The area around one and in which one moves.

SPATIAL ORIENTATION: Ability to move one's body in a coordinated way among objects within the environment.

SPLINTER SKILL: A motor skill limited and developed to a high degree without integration or unrelated to a total movement pattern.

TACTUAL: Sensations from the sense of touch; external contact sensation.

TIME: The rate or speed of movement.

VESTIBULAR SYSTEM: The sensory system that responds to the position of the head in relation to gravity and accelerated or decelerated movement.

VISUAL-MOTOR: An accurate match between eye movements and movements of other muscle groups of the body (often referred to as hand-eye or foot-eye).

144

APPENDIX C

WEEKLY ACTIVITY PLAN

Movement Skill Area:_____   Date:_____
Curriculum Theme:_____   Teacher:_____
Purpose:

Procedure:

Materials:

Number of Students:_____
Comments (positive & suggested improvements for the activity):

Suggestions for future activities with this Movement Skill Area:

APPENDIX D

BASIC SKILLS REINFORCEMENT CLASSLIST

CLASS:_____

DATE:_____

CHILDREN WHO NEED SPECIAL HELP WITH A SPECIFIC SKILL:	ACTIVITY FOR SKILL REINFORCEMENT:

BEAN BAG DIRECTIONS

1. For each bean bag pattern, make a set of 3 or 4 bean bags. These should be double stitched to prevent spillage.
2. Each set of 3-4 bean bags should weigh the same, so that the child can have a constant weight to throw and can vary the amount of effort he/she needs to use in throwing the bean bag a certain distance.
3. Bean bag sets should weigh between 3-5 ounces, with <u>all</u> of one set weighing the same amount.
4. Suggestions for bean bag sets:
   a. Use patterns found in young children's coloring books.
   b. Make bags of different shapes (circle, triangle, square, rectangle).
   c. Use fabric of different colors (red, blue, green, yellow).
   d. Use fabric of different textures (cordury, velvet, kettlecloth).
   e. Fill bags with different materials (sand, rice, beans, peas, gravel-- If a set is filled with different materials, be sure <u>all</u> bean bags weigh the same).
   f. Make bean bags which will reinforce the curriculum unit (bats for Halloween, birds for spring, eggs for food unit).
5. Refer to pages 96 & 97 for rationale.

WOODEN GEOMETRIC SHAPE DIRECTIONS

1. Make shapes out of 3/8" plywood.
2. Cut the shapes with 3" wide edges.
3. Keep cutting the same shape out of the center of the larger shape until ending up with a small solid shape. (Getting 3 hollow & 1 solid of each shape.)
4. Round edges by sanding very thoroughally.
5. Prime and paint 2 coats with enamel. Vary the colors so that there is one shape of each color for each size (see chart below).

6. <u>Outer dimensions</u> for each shape and <u>color chart</u>:

CIRCLE		SQUARE		TRIANGLE		RECTANGLE	
red	30"	blue	30"	yellow	40"	green	30"x36"
b	24"	y	24"	g	33"	r	24"x30"
y	18"	g	18"	r	26"	b	18"x24"
g	12"	r	12"	b	19"	y	12"x18"

7. Stand: Spray with clear finish after sanding smoothly.

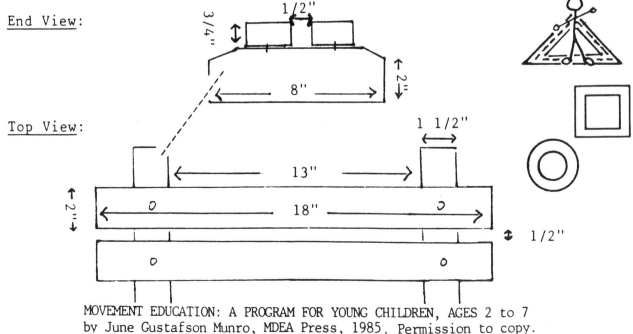

End View:

Top View:

MOVEMENT EDUCATION: A PROGRAM FOR YOUNG CHILDREN, AGES 2 to 7
by June Gustafson Munro, MDEA Press, 1985. Permission to copy.

INDEX